Britain Explored

NEW EDITION

Paul Harvey

Rhodri Jones

www.longman.com

Contents

1

The Geography of Britain

(above left) *A village of stone-built houses in Yorkshire* (right) *Scottish moorland in winter*
(below left) *Brighton in summer* (right) *The rush hour in London*

◾ Highland and lowland Britain ◾

Britain is unpredictable in climate and varied in scenery. In particular, there is a dramatic contrast between 'highland' and 'lowland' Britain. The differences between the two areas affect many aspects of people's lives.

The most precise distinction is geological. The rocks of most of the north and west of Great Britain are harder and older than those of the south and east. These older rocks are covered by large areas of moorland such as the Lake District, the Pennines and much of Scotland and Wales, where the soils are poor, thin and stony. In addition, these areas are wetter and harder to reach than the lower land to the south and east. As a result, these

areas of the British Isles are thinly populated except where coal or iron have been discovered. Most of the coalfields, which were the home of the industrial revolution, lie along the dividing line between highland and lowland Britain.

The south and east are rarely flat, but instead of high continuous moorland there are bands of hills which alternate with areas of lowland. The soils are generally deeper and richer, and the climate is drier and better suited to farming. Industry benefits from easier communications. Thus human settlement in these areas is dense and more evenly spread.

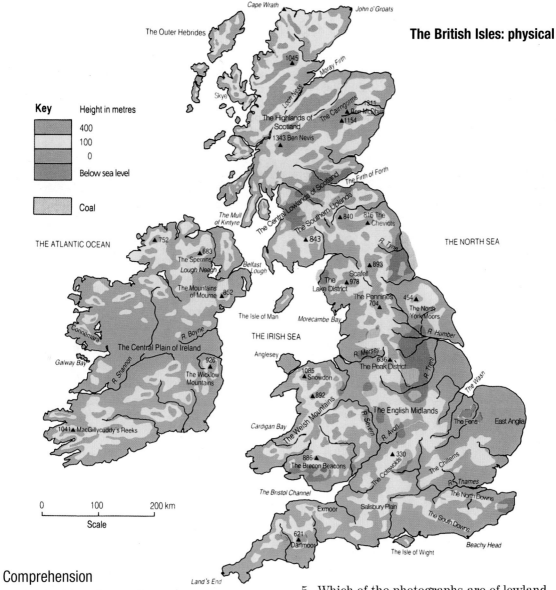

The British Isles: physical

Key — Height in metres
400
100
0
Below sea level

Coal

Comprehension

Use the information on these
two pages to answer the questions.

1 Where is the highest mountain in Britain?
2 What is 'moorland'? Find an example on
  the map.
3 Which of these areas have coalfields: South
  Wales, Central Scotland, The Fens, The
  Thames Valley, Northern Ireland?
4 Which of these expressions describe
  highland Britain: *drier, more difficult to
  reach, more thinly populated, better for
  farming, more mountainous?*

5 Which of the photographs are of lowland
  Britain?

Discussion

Work in pairs.

1 Decide which is the most important
  geographical difference between highland
  and lowland Britain.
2 Compare Britain with your own country.
  Which are the most obvious geographical
  differences?

■ Population ■

Although Britain is densely populated, there are large areas which contain fewer than 100 people per square kilometre (for example, much of Scotland, Wales and Northern Ireland). Densities of more than 500 people per square kilometre are only found in the main industrial areas (such as the Midlands and South-East England). There are only five cities with populations over 500,000, although Manchester, Liverpool and Newcastle also exceed this figure if neighbouring towns are included.

EUROPE: POPULATION			
Country	Area (km^2)	Population	Density per km^2
United Kingdom	242,900	58,784,000	242
Other members of the European Union			
Austria	83,859	8,072,000	96
Belgium	30,528	10,188,000	334
Denmark	43,094	5,284,000	123
Finland	338,145	5,140,000	15
France	551,500	58,607,000	106
Germany	357,022	82,071,000	230
Greece	131,957	10,256,464	78
Ireland	70,273	3,626,087	52
Italy	301,318	57,523,000	191
Luxembourg	2,586	417,000	161
Netherlands	41,526	15,604,000	376
Portugal	91,982	9,920,760	108
Spain	505,992	39,270,000	78
Sweden	449,964	8,846,000	20
The world's extremes			
Mongolia	1,566,500	2,313,000	1
Hong Kong	1,075	6,687,200	6,221

Comprehension

Use the information on these two pages to answer the questions.

1 Name some cities in Britain with large populations. Which is the furthest from the sea?
2 How far is it from London to Edinburgh: 350, 500 or 650 km? Name a town that is a similar distance from the capital city of your own country.
3 Which countries in Western Europe are bigger than Britain? Which are more densely populated than Britain?
4 Which three countries in the table have the lowest densities of population?

Discussion

Work in pairs.

1 Name some of the thinly populated areas of Britain.
2 Write a few short sentences to describe the distribution of population in your own country.

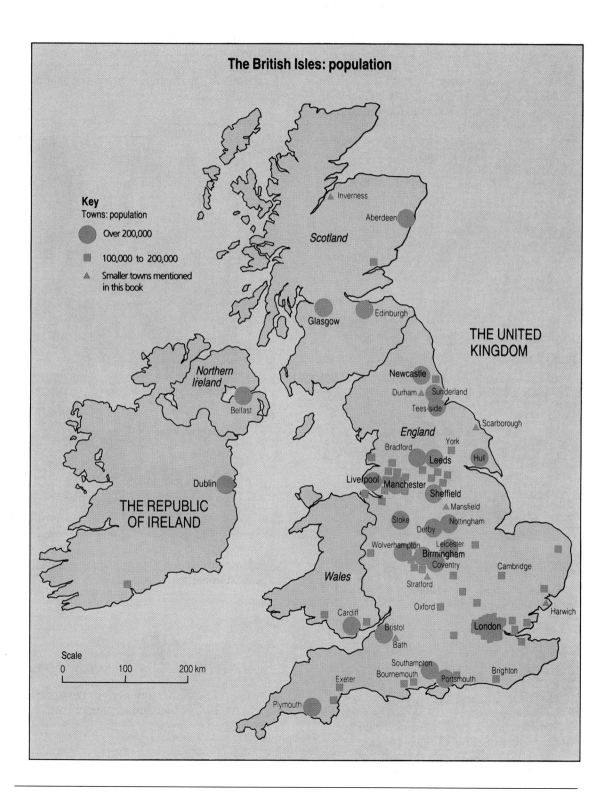

The British Isles: population

Key
Towns: population

● Over 200,000

■ 100,000 to 200,000

▲ Smaller towns mentioned in this book

Inverness

Aberdeen

Scotland

Glasgow

Edinburgh

THE UNITED KINGDOM

Northern Ireland

Belfast

Newcastle

Durham Sunderland

Tees-side

Scarborough

England

Bradford York

Leeds Hull

Liverpool Manchester

Sheffield

Mansfield

Dublin

THE REPUBLIC OF IRELAND

Stoke

Derby Nottingham

Wolverhampton Leicester

Birmingham

Coventry Cambridge

Stratford

Wales

Oxford

Harwich

Cardiff

London

Bristol

Bath

Southampton

Exeter Bournemouth Portsmouth Brighton

Plymouth

Scale

0   100   200 km

■ The weather ■

Britain is as far north as Canada's Hudson Bay or Siberia. For example Edinburgh is 56 degrees north of the equator, the same latitude as Moscow, yet its climate is much milder because of the Gulf Stream, which brings warm water and air across the Atlantic from the Gulf of Mexico. As a result, snow only falls occasionally and does not remain for long, except in the Scottish mountains, where skiing is possible. Average temperatures in England and Wales vary from 4°C in January to 16°C in July and August. In Scotland averages are one or two degrees cooler, and an average July day is about as warm as Marseilles in December.

The wind brings rain from the Atlantic to the hills of the west. This means that the western parts of Britain are wetter than the east, which is fairly sheltered. London is drier than continental cities such as Hamburg. Its weather may be unpredictable, but it is not particularly wet.

Annual rainfall

Monthly rainfall

Scotland

England and Wales

Key
In one recent year
Average over 30 years

0   100   200 km

Key
Over 1,500 mm
750 mm–1,500 mm
Under 750 mm

■ Land use ■

Over three-quarters of Britain's land is used for farming, but less than 2 per cent of the working population work on farms. These farms produce nearly half of the food that Britain needs, including 85 per cent of its wheat, nearly all of its milk and eggs, and nearly half of its sugar.

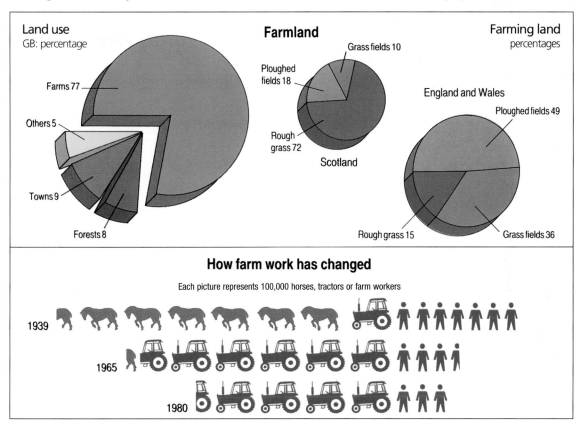

Land use
GB: percentage

Farms 77

Others 5

Towns 9

Forests 8

Farmland

Grass fields 10

Ploughed fields 18

Rough grass 72

Scotland

Farming land
percentages

England and Wales

Ploughed fields 49

Rough grass 15

Grass fields 36

How farm work has changed

Each picture represents 100,000 horses, tractors or farm workers

1939

1965

1980

Comprehension

Use the information on these two pages to answer the questions.

1 Why is Britain warmer than other countries on the same latitude?
2 Why do cities like Birmingham get their water from Wales?
3 What kind of food does Britain import from other countries?
4 Why do you think farming has become lonely work in Britain?

Discussion

Work in pairs.

1 Compare the annual rainfall map with the map on page 7 and decide which of these towns are in the drier half of Britain: Glasgow, Scarborough, Brighton, Cardiff, Edinburgh, Harwich, Plymouth, Leicester, Liverpool.

2 What is the difference between farms in Scotland and farms in England and Wales? Find any information in this unit which helps to explain the difference.

3 If you were planning a holiday in Britain, how useful would average monthly rainfall statistics be?

■ Walking through Britain ■

Introduction

The speaker has walked from John o'Groats to Land's End.

1 How far is it according to the physical map on page 5?
2 Choose a walking route from John o'Groats to Land's End and list five places you would visit.
3 List five towns on the direct route, from the population map on page 7.

Listening

1 Listen to the first part of the tape and follow the route on the physical map.
   a Which places on the map does he mention?
   b Which mountain did he climb?
   c Which river did he cross?
2 What was the weather like in Wales?
3 What differences are there between your route and his?

4 Listen to the second part of the tape and follow the route on the population map.
   a Which places on the map does he mention?
   b Put these motorways in the order in which he mentions them: M1, M4, M6.
5 Which motorway goes from London to the west?
6 Is his route more direct than yours?

Discussion

Work in pairs.

1 Listen again and match each place with a person or activity.
   a Glasgow
   b Lake District
   c Exmoor
   d West coast of Scotland
   e Plymouth

   1 sailing
   2 Charles Rennie Mackintosh, architect
   3 Sir Francis Drake, Elizabethan sailor
   4 William Wordsworth
   5 pony trekking

2 Which place on the tape sounds most attractive to you? Why?

■ Summary ■

Vocabulary

1 Make five two-word expressions from the list, each matching one of the five items below:

soil population city rainfall stony density mountain midland distribution scenery

a Birmingham or Leicester, for example.
b The number of people per square kilometre.
c How wet the weather is in different places.
d Why tourists visit Scotland and North Wales.
e Why farmers have problems in Scotland and North Wales.

2 Work in pairs.

a Which of the following words would you associate with (i) Scotland, (ii) London or (iii) Brighton? Explain your reasons.

skiing summer coal tractors holiday traffic government seaside mountains scenery capital densely sunshine

b Which of the above words would you associate with towns or regions in your own country?

Discussion

Imagine you have to live in one of the following places: Cardiff, Edinburgh, the Lake District, Bournemouth, Birmingham, Liverpool, the Cotswolds or John o'Groats.

1 Find the eight places on the maps.
2 Find as much information as you can about each place, including its weather, its distance from London, the size if it is a town, and the sort of scenery you would find nearby. Keep notes to use below in *Writing*.
3 Decide which place you would prefer to live in.

4 Discuss your choice with any other students who have chosen the same place and make a list of all your reasons for living there.
5 List all the reasons for not living in the other places.

Writing

Use the notes you have made above.

1 Write a short paragraph comparing the south and east of Britain with the north and west.
2 Imagine you have a British pen-friend who has never visited your country. Choose your favourite place in your own country and write a short letter to your pen-friend describing it.

Snowdonia, Wales

2

The United Kingdom

■ Great Britain and The United Kingdom ■

Bonnie Prince Charlie

British passport

The Prince of Wales

Strictly speaking, 'Great Britain' is a geographical expression but 'The United Kingdom' is a political expression. Great Britain is in fact the biggest of the group of islands which lie between the North Sea and the Atlantic Ocean. It is approximately two and a half times the size of Ireland, the second largest. Together they are called the British Isles. The expression originally described the islands themselves, not the political or national divisions within them.

The British Isles today are shared by two separate and independent states. The smaller of these is the Republic of Ireland, with its capital in Dublin. The larger, with London as its capital, is the United Kingdom of Great Britain and Northern Ireland. This long title, (usually shortened to the United Kingdom or UK) is the result of a complicated history.

The island of Great Britain contains three 'nations' which were separate at earlier stages of their history: England, Scotland and Wales. Wales had become part of the English administrative system by the sixteenth century. Scotland was not completely united with England until 1707. The United Kingdom is a name which was introduced in 1801 when Great Britain became united with Ireland. When the Republic of Ireland became independent of London in 1922, the title was changed to its present form.

'Britain' and 'British' have two meanings. They sometimes refer to Great Britain alone, and sometimes to the UK including Northern Ireland. 'England' and 'English' are often incorrectly used to refer to the whole of Great Britain.

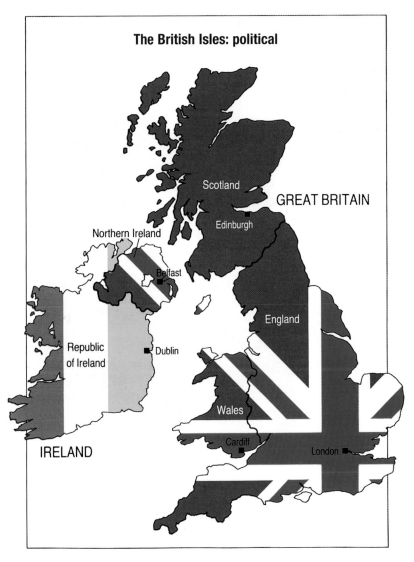

The British Isles: political

GREAT BRITAIN

Scotland

Edinburgh

Northern Ireland

Belfast

England

Republic
of Ireland

Dublin

Wales

IRELAND

Cardiff

London

Comprehension

Use the information on these two pages to answer the questions.

1 Explain the differences between these expressions: Great Britain, the United Kingdom, the Republic of Ireland, the British Isles. What did 'the United Kingdom' originally refer to?

2 Which of these people are British: an Englishman, a citizen of the Irish Republic, a Scot, a Welshman?

3 Which of these capital cities are the capitals of independent states: Edinburgh, Belfast, Dublin, Cardiff, London?

4 An Irishman might not agree that he lives in the British Isles. Why not?

Discussion

Work in pairs.

1 Make notes on the physical geography of England, Scotland and Wales. Look back through Unit 1 if necessary.

2 Using your notes and the information on these two pages, prepare a short description of the physical differences between England, Scotland and Wales.

THE BRITISH ISLES: POPULATION			
Country	Area (km^2)	Population	Density per km^2
England	130,410	48,903,000	375
Scotland	78,789	5,137,000	65
Wales	20,758	2,917,000	141
Northern Ireland	14,160	1,649,000	116
Republic of Ireland	70,273	3,626,087	52

■ Scotland and Wales ■

Scottish history

There were constant wars between England and the quite separate Kingdom of Scotland from the eleventh to the sixteenth centuries. Here are some important events in Scottish history:

1603 James VI of Scotland became also James I of England when Queen Elizabeth I of England died without children.

1651 Scotland was united with England and Wales although it kept its own parliament.

1707 England and Scotland were joined by an Act of Union which abolished the Scottish parliament.

1715 and **1745** Rebellions by 'Jacobites' who wanted a Catholic king. The English parliament had invited the Dutch Protestant William of Orange to rule Britain. In 1745 the Jacobite hope was Prince Charles Edward Stuart, 'Bonny Prince Charlie'.

1746 Bonny Prince Charlie was finally defeated at Culloden, near Inverness. The people of the Highlands were forced to emigrate to make room for sheep farms. Today there are twenty million 'overseas Scots'.

Today Since 1999 Scotland has had its own parliament in Edinburgh, with a wide range of responsibilities such as education and health.

Scottish Parliament

Welsh National Assembly

Welsh history

1301 After defeating the native princes of Wales, King Edward I of England named his son 'Prince of Wales'. Since then the eldest son of the king or queen of England has traditionally been given this title.

1536 Wales was brought into the English system of national and local government by an Act of Union.

1850 South Wales became heavily industrialised in the nineteenth century.

Today Since 1999 Wales has had its own National Assembly in Cardiff.

Welsh and Gaelic

Most of Britain was inhabited by Celts until the fourth century. Their languages were not related to English. In the fourth century the Anglo-Saxons invaded Britain from Northern Germany and Denmark, and their language formed the basis of the English we speak today. The Anglo-Saxons drove the Celts into the mountainous west of Britain. Two Celtic languages survive there: Welsh and Gaelic.

Welsh is spoken by half a million people, 20 per cent of the population of Wales. The western counties of Wales are at least 50 per cent Welsh-speaking. Welsh and English are both used in official contexts in Wales.

Gaelic is used in the Republic of Ireland, where it is the first official language, and in Scotland. Although over a million people claim some knowledge of Irish Gaelic, it is habitually spoken by only about 15,000 people in the far west of Ireland. Scots Gaelic is spoken by 80,000 people in the hills and islands of the west of Scotland, but it has no official status.

Nearly all Welsh and Gaelic speakers are bilingual, although most would think of English as their second language.

Road signs in English and Welsh

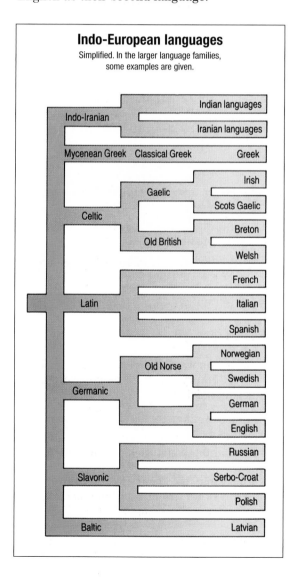

Indo-European languages

Simplified. In the larger language families, some examples are given.

- Indo-Iranian
  - Indian languages
  - Iranian languages
- Mycenean Greek — Classical Greek — Greek
- Celtic
  - Gaelic
    - Irish
    - Scots Gaelic
  - Old British
    - Breton
    - Welsh
- Latin
  - French
  - Italian
  - Spanish
- Germanic
  - Old Norse
    - Norwegian
    - Swedish
  - German
  - English
- Slavonic
  - Russian
  - Serbo-Croat
  - Polish
- Baltic
  - Latvian

Comprehension

Use the information on these two pages to answer the following questions.

1 When did Scotland and Wales start being governed from London?
2 Prince Charles is 'Prince of Wales'. Where does this title come from?
3 Which country do you think is more independent of England: Scotland or Wales?
4 Which Celtic language in the British Isles has the largest number of native speakers today?

Discussion

Work in pairs.

1 Scotland and Wales remain different from England in some ways. Find examples and reasons for this in Units 1 and 2.
2 Does everyone speak the same language in your country? Describe any differences in language or dialect.

■ Ireland ■

Irish history

1155 King Henry II of England was made King of all Ireland by the Pope. There were still native Irish Kings of parts of Ireland.

1541 King Henry VIII of England, self-declared head of a new English Protestant church, was recognised as King of Ireland by the English parliament. Later, his daughter Elizabeth I broke the power of the Irish kings. She was afraid they would help Catholic Spain in its war against England.

1609 In a further move against Irish Catholics, their land was given to tens of thousands of Protestants from England and the Scottish Lowlands. Ulster (modern Northern Ireland) soon had more Protestants than Catholics.

1689 The Dutch Protestant William of Orange had been invited by the English parliament to become King of England instead of the current king, James II, who was a Catholic. James still claimed to be King of Ireland, but the Protestants in Ulster fought against him.

1690 William of Orange finally defeated James II in Ireland at the Battle of the Boyne. Since then there has been no Catholic king or queen in Britain.

1703 By this time, only 14 per cent of Irish land was still owned by Catholics. In Ulster, Protestants owned 95 per cent of the land.

1800 Act of Union between Great Britain and Ireland.

1845–1849 The Great Famine. Repeated failure of the Irish potato harvest caused death and suffering. Between 1840 and 1900, the population of Ireland fell from 8.5 million to 4.5 million. Two million people emigrated to the United States, Canada and Australia. In the same period, the population of England doubled (from 16 million to 32 million).

1916 The Easter Rising. Irish nationalists rebelled during the First World War (1914–1918). Three years of bitter fighting followed. The Irish nationalist party Sinn Fein (Gaelic for 'Ourselves Alone') developed a military wing, the Irish Republican Army (IRA).

1922 Partition of Ireland. The Catholic South became the Irish Free State (later the Irish Republic), with its parliament in Dublin. The Protestant North continued to be part of the United Kingdom, but with its own local parliament in Belfast.

1969 The British Army was sent to Northern Ireland after disturbances between Protestants and Catholics.

1972 Direct rule from London replaced the Northern Irish Parliament.

1998 The Good Friday Agreement was signed between the British and Irish governments and the political parties in Northern Ireland to create an elected National Assembly for Northern Ireland, including representatives of both the Protestant and the Catholic communities. The Assembly did not function until May 2000, after the IRA had agreed to follow its nationalist policies peacefully.

Comprehension

Use the information on these two pages to answer the questions.

1 Are Catholics or Protestants in the majority in (a) Northern Ireland and (b) the Republic of Ireland?
2 When did the current British Army presence in Northern Ireland begin?
3 What is the IRA?
4 What does the poster advise people to do?

Discussion

Work in pairs.

1 Find any similarities between the history of Ireland and the histories of Scotland or Wales.
2 Is it possible to compare Northern Ireland with any other troubled parts of the world?

STAY ALIVE
BREAK YOUR ROUTINE

SECTARIAN MURDER MUST BE
STOPPED. YOU CAN HELP TO MAKE
NORTHERN IRELAND A SAFER PLACE
FOR YOU AND YOUR FAMILY.

IF YOU HAVE ANY INFORMATION
RING THE CONFIDENTIAL TELEPHONE

BELFAST 652155

Issued by The Security Forces

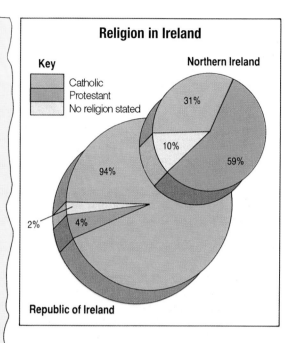

Religion in Ireland

Key
- Catholic
- Protestant
- No religion stated

Northern Ireland

31%

10%

59%

94%

2%

4%

Republic of Ireland

Security poster in Northern Ireland

DON'T BECOME A VICTIM OF TIME

MONDAY	TUESDAY	WEDNESDAY	THURSDAY

HOME AT 6.30	HOME AT 6.30	HOME AT 6.30	HOME AT 6.30

FRIDAY

DEAD AT 6.30

■ Northern Ireland ■

Introduction

1 Write one sentence describing your own image of Northern Ireland.
2 Put these words from the tape in groups of three under the headings (a), (b) and (c) below:

   riots unemployment danger
   depression hospitality bombings
   optimism night life housing problems

   a 'The Troubles': conflict in Northern Ireland
   b The legacy: long term effects of the Troubles
   c Encouragement: the positive aspects

Listening

1 Where did the speaker grow up?
   a Manchester
   b Bangor, County Down
   c Belfast
2 Where does she live now?

3 Why did she move?
4 Why does she think other people move?
5 What does she remember from her schooldays?
6 How have things changed now?
   a Is life more or less dangerous?
   b How has Belfast changed?
7 How often does she go back?

Discussion

Work in pairs.

1 In what ways do you think Northern Irish attitudes might be different from English attitudes on these subjects:
   a abortion?
   b smoking?
   c drinking and driving?
2 Which of the speaker's points would encourage you or discourage you from visiting Northern Ireland?

■ Summary ■

Vocabulary

1 Define the following words, using a dictionary if necessary:
   emigration overseas dialect region district capital visitor
   battle population industry

2 Complete the following table.

Country	Nationality	Language(s)	Person
			a Briton (rare)
		English Scots Gaelic	
	Welsh		
Ireland			

Discussion

1 Which of the words in *Vocabulary 1* unite people, which divide them, and which both unite and divide?
2 Make lists of things which have helped to unite and divide the UK.
3 Work in pairs. Compare the things on your lists and decide which of them are most important today. Discuss your points with the rest of the class.

Writing

Imagine you are describing your own country to a foreign visitor. Which things unite and divide your own people today? Write a short description which would help a foreign visitor to understand your country.

3

The Constitution

■ The system of government ■

In theory, the constitution has three branches: Parliament, which makes laws, the Government, which 'executes' laws i.e. puts them into effect, and the law courts, which interpret laws. Although the Queen is officially head of all three branches, she has little direct power.

Parliament has two parts: the House of Commons and the House of Lords. Members of the House of Commons are elected by the voters of about 650 constituencies. They are known as MPs, or Members of Parliament. (The election system is described in Unit 4.) The Prime Minister, or leader of the Government, is also an MP, usually the leader of the political party with a majority in the House of Commons.

The Prime Minister is advised by a Cabinet of about twenty other ministers. The Cabinet includes the ministers in charge of major government departments or ministries. Departments and ministries are run by civil servants, who are permanent officials. Even if the Government changes after an election, the same civil servants are employed.

Members of the House of Lords (peers) are not elected at present. Until 1999 they were mostly 'hereditary peers' because their fathers had been peers before them. Now only 91 out of about 700 peers are hereditary: the rest are 'life peers' who cannot pass on their titles, senior judges (Law Lords) and Church of England Archbishops and Bishops.

The Queen opening Parliament, with Prince Philip

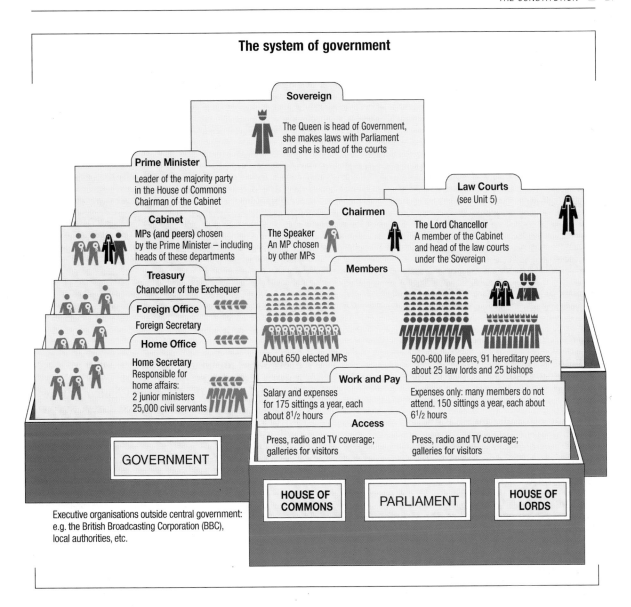

The system of government

Sovereign
The Queen is head of Government, she makes laws with Parliament and she is head of the courts

Prime Minister
Leader of the majority party in the House of Commons
Chairman of the Cabinet

Law Courts
(see Unit 5)

Cabinet
MPs (and peers) chosen by the Prime Minister – including heads of these departments

Chairmen

The Speaker
An MP chosen by other MPs

The Lord Chancellor
A member of the Cabinet and head of the law courts under the Sovereign

Treasury
Chancellor of the Exchequer

Members

Foreign Office
Foreign Secretary

Home Office
Home Secretary
Responsible for home affairs:
2 junior ministers
25,000 civil servants

About 650 elected MPs

500-600 life peers, 91 hereditary peers, about 25 law lords and 25 bishops

Work and Pay
Salary and expenses for 175 sittings a year, each about 8¹/2 hours

Expenses only: many members do not attend. 150 sittings a year, each about 6¹/2 hours

Access
Press, radio and TV coverage; galleries for visitors

Press, radio and TV coverage; galleries for visitors

GOVERNMENT

Executive organisations outside central government: e.g. the British Broadcasting Corporation (BBC), local authorities, etc.

HOUSE OF COMMONS

PARLIAMENT

HOUSE OF LORDS

Comprehension

Use the information on these two pages to answer the questions.

1 Which of these people are not elected: a peer, an MP, a civil servant, the Prime Minister?
2 What is the difference between a life peer and a hereditary peer?
3 What are civil servants?
4 Which areas of government do these people deal with: the Chancellor of the Exchequer, the Home Secretary, the Lord Chancellor?
5 Find two examples of executive organisations outside central government.

Discussion

Work in pairs.

1 What differences are there between Parliament and the Government?
2 List some similarities and differences between the UK parliamentary system and your own.

Parliament

The Palace of Westminster

Functions of parliament

- making laws
- providing money for government, through taxation
- examining government policy, administration and spending
- debating political questions.

Making new laws: Bills and Acts

A proposal for a new law is called a bill. Bills may be introduced in either the House of Commons or the House of Lords by any member. In practice most bills are proposed by the Government. After being discussed and perhaps changed, the bill is sent to the other House to go through the same process. When both Houses agree on a text, the bill is sent to the Queen for her signature (or 'Royal Assent') at which point it becomes an Act of Parliament. A bill which has been passed by the House of Commons is almost certain to become law, and about fifty bills become Acts each year. The House of Lords can revise bills but it cannot stop them from becoming Acts; it can only delay the process. The Royal Assent is a formality: no sovereign has refused a bill since 1707.

Many countries have a written constitution like that of the United States. Because this is not the case in Britain, there are no special procedures for changing the laws which govern the country. If a political party has a clear majority in the House of Commons it can make new laws and give itself new powers. This allows a Government to make radical changes in the law.

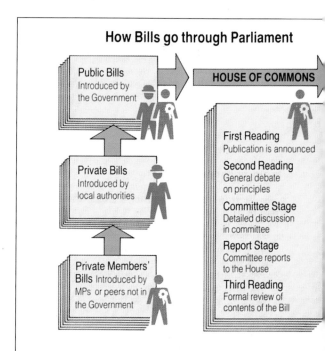

How Bills go through Parliament

Public Bills
Introduced by the Government

Private Bills
Introduced by local authorities

Private Members' Bills Introduced by MPs or peers not in the Government

HOUSE OF COMMONS

First Reading
Publication is announced

Second Reading
General debate on principles

Committee Stage
Detailed discussion in committee

Report Stage
Committee reports to the House

Third Reading
Formal review of contents of the Bill

■ The Government ■

Functions of the Prime Minister

- leading the majority party
- running the Government
- appointing Cabinet Ministers and other ministers
- representing the nation in political matters.

The Cabinet

Since the eighteenth century the Cabinet has been increasingly responsible for deciding policies and controlling and coordinating government administration. It meets in private and its discussions are secret. When a policy has been decided, an individual minister must either support it or resign, because the Cabinet acts as one body with 'collective responsibility'.

The Prime Minister has considerable individual power to introduce and control policies, and to change the Cabinet by appointing new ministers, sacking old ones, or 'reshuffling' the Cabinet by moving its members to other Cabinet posts.

10 Downing Street, the Prime Minister's London residence

Comprehension

Use the information on these two pages to answer the questions.

1 Name two functions of Parliament and two of the Prime Minister.
2 What is the difference between the constitutions of the United Kingdom and the United States?
3 Which of the two Houses of Parliament has more power?
4 What is the difference between a Bill and an Act of Parliament?
5 What is 'collective responsibility'?

Discussion

Work in pairs.

1 If the Prime Minister wants to introduce a new law, what do the following do: the Cabinet, the House of Commons, the House of Lords, the Queen?
2 Make a list of features of the British constitution which you consider important and compare them with the constitution of your own country.

HOUSE OF LORDS	ROYAL ASSENT

If the Bill has been introduced in the Commons, it is then reviewed in the Lords. Some Bills start in the Lords and then go to the Commons.

The Lords have less formal methods of debating Bills. They can delay but not stop a Bill.

The Bill is signed by the Queen and becomes law.

The Royal Assent is still read out in Parliament in Norman-French: 'La reyne le veult.'

■ The Sovereign ■

'Her Most Excellent Majesty Elizabeth the Second by the Grace of God, of the United Kingdom of Great Britain and Northern Ireland and of Her other Realms and Territories Queen, Head of the Commonwealth, Defender of the Faith.'

The Queen is the official Head of State and, for many people, a symbol of the unity of the nation. For a thousand years England (and later the whole of the United Kingdom) has been united under one sovereign, a continuity broken only after the Civil War, by the republic of 1649 to 1660. The Crown is passed to the sovereign's eldest son, although in future it will pass to the eldest child, whether son or daughter.

The Queen has a central role in state affairs, not only through her ceremonial functions, such as opening Parliament, but also because she meets the Prime Minister every week and receives copies of all Cabinet papers. However, she is expected to be impartial or 'above politics', and any advice she may offer the Prime Minister is kept secret.

Functions of the Sovereign

- opening Parliament
- approving the appointment of the Prime Minister
- giving her Royal Assent to bills
- giving honours such as peerages, knighthoods and medals
- Head of the Commonwealth
- Head of the Church of England
- Commander-in-Chief of the armed forces.

■ The Royal Family ■

Many members of the Royal Family undertake official duties in Britain and abroad. Their various responsibilities reflect tradition, their own personal interests and Britain's former imperial status. For example, among her many titles the Princess Royal (Princess Anne) is Chancellor of the University of London, Colonel-in-Chief of eleven Army regiments, including the 8th Canadian Hussars and the Royal New Zealand Nursing Corps, and president of the Save the Children Fund, for whom she has travelled widely.

The Royal Family's money comes from two sources: government funds and their own personal wealth, which is considerable. On the one hand the Queen is certainly one of the richest women in the world, while on the other her power is limited by the fact that so many of her expenses are paid for by government money. Parliament has had effective control of the monarch's finances since the seventeenth century.

A survey in 1989 found that 71 per cent of people in Britain thought that the Royal Family offered value for money – this was fewer than in previous surveys. As many as 74 per cent thought the younger Royals should 'get proper jobs'.

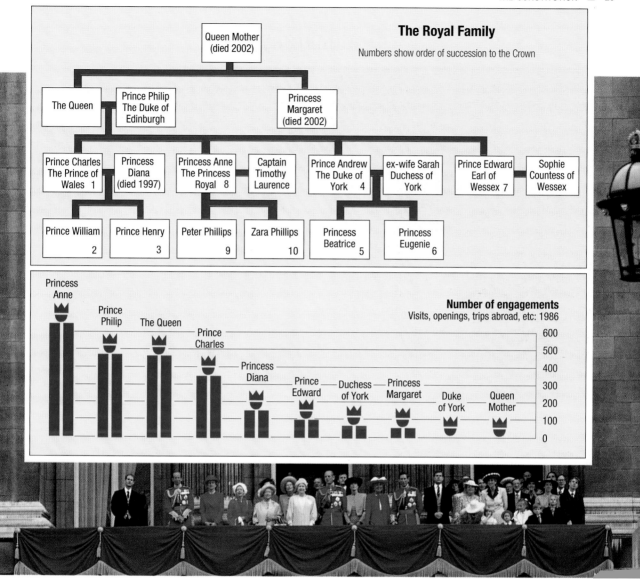

The Royal Family

Numbers show order of succession to the Crown

Number of engagements
Visits, openings, trips abroad, etc: 1986

Comprehension

Use the information on these two pages to answer the questions.

1 Who is next in line to the British crown after Prince Charles?
2 How can Parliament control the Royal Family?
3 What connections can you find between the Royal Family and the world outside Britain?
4 Which member of the Royal Family has the highest number of public engagements?

Discussion

Work in pairs.

1 Which members of the British Royal Family are best known in your own country? Why?
2 What powers does the Queen have in government?
3 Do you think being a member of the Royal Family is a 'proper job'? What sort of work do they do?

■ Monarchy ■

Introduction

1 List four countries which have monarchies.
2 Which of these adjectives do you associate
   with the British monarch:
   ostentatious greedy modest vulgar
   wealthy lazy dignified popular
   hard-working?

Listening

1 Does the speaker approve:
   a of the British monarchy?
   b of monarchies in general?
2 How does he compare monarchs and
   presidents?
3 Which monarchies does he praise? Why?
4 Does he feel sorry for the British Royal
   Family?
5 How does he compare monarchs and 'soap
   operas' (popular television dramas)?
6 Which of the adjectives in the *Introduction*
   does he associate with the British
   monarchy? Is your own list different?

7 Listen again and complete the quotations
   from the tape.
   a I used to . . . . royal families in
     general.
   b I think now I . . . . the idea of a
     royal family.
   c I . . . . them personally, if you like.
   d I think I would . . . . a monarchy
     of the sort you find in other countries in
     Northern Europe.

Discussion

Work in pairs.

1 What do you see as the advantages and
   disadvantages of having a monarchy?
2 The speaker would 'swop my job for their
   job any day'.
   a Would you exchange lives with a member
     of the British Royal Family?
   b Why? (Why not?)
   c If so, which member would you swop
     with?

■ Summary ■

Vocabulary

1 Check the meanings of these twelve expressions from the unit. Make one sentence from each set of words, using them in any order, to describe the British system.
   a MPs   election   House of Commons
   b Prime Minister   ministers   Cabinet
   c majority   House of Lords   hereditary
   d bill   Royal Assent   Act of Parliament

2 Turn the following nouns into adjectives:
   constitution   ceremony   politics
   administration   empire   royalty

Discussion

Look at the diagram on page 21. It shows a division of powers which is found in most constitutional systems.

1 Does the diagram show where real power lies in Britain?
2 What changes would you make to the diagram to represent the system in your own country?
3 Look up any words you would need to describe your system in English.

Writing

Write a description of the constitutional system of your own country. Use the text on page 20 as a model.

Peers in regalia at the house of Lords

4

Politics

■ The political system ■

The United Kingdom is divided into 650 parliamentary constituencies, each with an electorate of about 60,000 voters. Each British citizen over eighteen has the vote (although voting is not compulsory). Each constituency is represented by one Member of Parliament in the House of Commons.

Any number of candidates can stand for election in each constituency. The main political parties are usually represented, and sometimes candidates representing minority parties also stand. The winner is the candidate who gets more votes than any other single candidate, even if the difference is only one vote. This 'first past the post' system is clear, familiar and simple, but it means that the candidate who comes second gets nothing. In 1987 for example, the Liberal/SDP Alliance received 23.1 per cent of the total vote but won only 22 seats (3.5 per cent) in Parliament.

The leader of the party with most seats becomes Prime Minister and forms a Government, which can remain in power for up to five years unless the Prime Minister decides to hold an earlier election. The second biggest party becomes the official Opposition. Its leader forms a 'Shadow Cabinet'. Since 1945 the Conservatives and Labour have been either the Government or the Opposition.

(below) *The House of Commons in session* (inset) *Prime Minister Tony Blair*

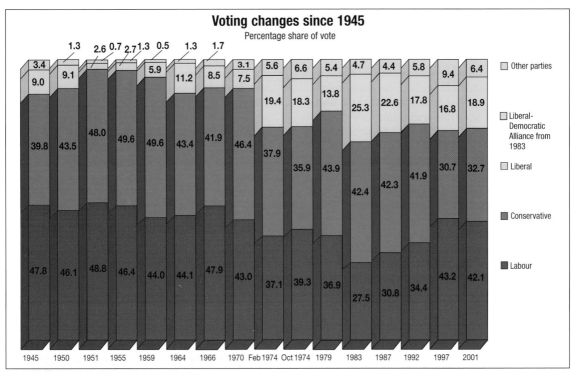

Voting changes since 1945

Percentage share of vote

Legend: Other parties | Liberal-Democratic Alliance from 1983 | Liberal | Conservative | Labour

Year	Other	Liberal/Alliance	Conservative	Labour
1945	3.4	9.0	39.8	47.8
1950	1.3	9.1	43.5	46.1
1951	2.6		48.0	48.8
1955	0.7		49.6	46.4
1959	2.7	5.9	49.6	44.0
1964	1.3	11.2	43.4	44.1
1966	0.5	8.5	41.9	47.9
1970	1.3	7.5	46.4	43.0
Feb 1974	1.7	19.4	37.9	37.1
Oct 1974	3.1	18.3	35.9	39.3
1979	5.6	13.8	43.9	36.9
1983	6.6	25.3	42.4	27.5
1987	5.4	22.6	42.3	30.8
1992	4.7	17.8	41.9	34.4
1997	4.4	16.8	30.7	43.2
2001	5.8 / 9.4	18.9	32.7	42.1

In the 1980s, British politics was dominated by Margaret Thatcher: she was Britain's first woman Prime Minister, leader of the ruling Conservative Party and the longest-serving Prime Minister in the 20th century. Under Thatcher, it was Conservative policy to return state-owned industries to private ownership, cut taxation and control inflation. In 1997 her successor John Major was beaten by Tony Blair of Labour.

Breaking Conservative and Labour dominance

In 1981 a new party was formed to try to break the dominance of Conservative and Labour. Some Conservative and Labour MPs left their own parties to join the new Social Democrats. The new party then agreed to fight elections in alliance with the small but long-established Liberals, forming the Alliance. Their problem, under the 'first past the post' system, was to turn their popular vote into parliamentary seats. In 1987 the two parties of the Alliance agreed to merge to form a new party, the Liberal Democrats, although some Social Democrats preferred to remain independent.

Comprehension

Use the information on these two pages to answer the questions.

1 Which are the two largest political parties?
2 Which new political party appeared in Britain during the 1980s?
3 Which party did Margaret Thatcher lead?
4 Which of her policies are mentioned?

Discussion

Work in pairs.

1 Find the following in this election result: the constituency, the size of the electorate, the candidates, the parties, the winner, the size of the majority.

Mansfield (Notts) *E. 66,764*	
J. A. Meale, Lab.	19,610
C. Hendry, C	19,554
B. Answer, S.D.P./All.	11,604
B. Marshall, Moderate Labour	1,580
Lab. maj.	56

2 What advantages and disadvantages are there in the 'first past the post' system?

■ New Labour ■

In 1994, Tony Blair became leader of the Labour Party, which he called 'New Labour'. By early 1997 Labour had won so many seats in by-elections that the parliamentary majority of the Conservatives had been removed. However, Labour was weakened by divisions within the party. For example, in 1995 there was a fierce debate over whether Labour, if elected to government, should return privatised industries to state ownership.

Blair organised his party to run a sophisticated election campaign before the general election in May 1997, which emphasised his own role as leader. Meanwhile, John Major's Conservative government was weakened by disunity over their attitude towards the European Union and accusations of corruption. May the 1st produced the greatest victory in the Labour Party's history. They achieved the largest parliamentary majority of any government since 1945.

Under the Labour government, referendums were run in Scotland, Wales and London. The voters supported the creation of stronger local government in these regions. This has resulted in regional governments whose policies will not always agree with those of the national government.

At the same time, some progress was made towards peace in Northern Ireland. The Republic of Ireland agreed to drop the commitment written into its constitution to reclaim the whole of Ireland, and Northern Ireland eventually found itself with a national assembly which for the first time included representatives of Sinn Fein and the Roman Catholic minority.

In October 1999, membership of the House of Lords was changed radically. Instead of being dominated by hereditary peers, less than 100 remained, while the majority of members were life peers. The long term future of the House of Lords had not been decided at that stage.

In many ways, the Labour government built on the policies of the Conservatives before them. No privatised industries were returned to public ownership in this period. There were continuing debates over the level of public services such as education, health and transport. Extra money was found for these services, but the levels of taxation were not increased. As a result of continuing good economic conditions, the number of people out of work declined significantly.

Two conflicting views of Britain

'Britain has come right by her own efforts. We trusted in the character and talents of our people. The British instinct is for choice and independence. Given the opportunities provided by Conservative policies, many more families now enjoy the pride of ownership – of homes, of shares, and of pensions. Together we are building One Nation of free, prosperous and responsible families and people. A Conservative dream is at last becoming a reality.'
(*The Conservative Party Manifesto 1987*)

'Britain is crying out for change. Only a Labour government can bring it about. Mending divisions, building new strengths will need determination and realistic priorities. Commonsense and the Common interest require that the Tory philosophy of selfishness and short-term gain is replaced by the democratic socialist philosophy of community and caring, of investment in people and in production.
(*The Labour Party Manifesto 1987*)

Labour and Conservative Manifestos 2001

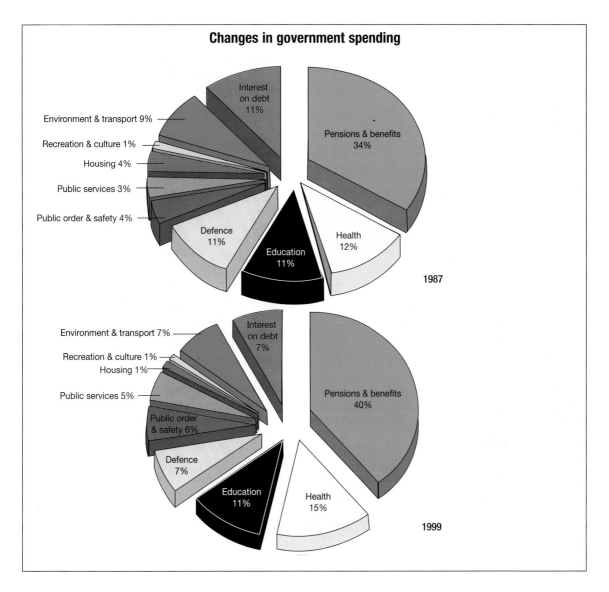

Changes in government spending

1987

- Interest on debt 11%
- Environment & transport 9%
- Recreation & culture 1%
- Housing 4%
- Public services 3%
- Public order & safety 4%
- Defence 11%
- Education 11%
- Health 12%
- Pensions & benefits 34%

1999

- Interest on debt 7%
- Environment & transport 7%
- Recreation & culture 1%
- Housing 1%
- Public services 5%
- Public order & safety 6%
- Defence 7%
- Education 11%
- Health 15%
- Pensions & benefits 40%

Comprehension

Use the information on these two pages to answer the questions.

1 What major events happened in these years: 1994, 1995, 1997, 1999?
2 What changes did the Labour government introduce in its first four years in power?
3 Which Conservative policy did Labour continue?
4 How did government spending change between 1987 and 1999? Which areas of spending increased and which decreased?

Discussion

Work in pairs.

1 Which is better in your view: central government or regional government?
2 How would you describe the differences between Conservative and Labour policy?
3 Can you find any ways in which changes in government spending reflect differences in policy?

■ General Election ■

From a Conservative Party leaflet

Crime: 'We would end Labour's early release programme which has allowed 23,000 prisoners back on to the street before half their sentences have been served.'

The National Health Service: 'We would encourage the growth of the private health sector for those who choose to use it.'

Transport: 'The railways are overcrowded, unreliable, dirty and expensive. Fuel prices have rocketed. We would invest in roads, make Railtrack carry out a proper investment programme and reduce the cost of fuel.'

Education: 'We believe that standards and funding should be administered by parents and governors rather than by Central Government.'

Europe: 'The Conservative party will fight the next election on a promise to keep the Pound Sterling, rather than adopt the Euro.'

From the Labour Party website

Crime: 'Crime doubled under the Conservatives. ... We are proud to be the first government in nearly half a century to go to the electorate with crime lower than when it entered office.'

The National Health Service: 'While we are modernising and investing in the NHS, the Tories' 'Patients' Guarantee' is a Trojan horse for the break-up of the NHS. So-called non-urgent operations such as hip operations would go to the back of the queue and the Tories would encourage people to go private and pay for their own operations.'

Transport: 'The transport system we inherited in 1997 was suffering from a huge investment backlog, ever increasing traffic congestion and crumbling roads. The Tories did not believe in public transport, and it showed.'

Education: 'Labour is delivering. ... The Tories' £16 billion cuts guarantee will hit schools hard. Their 'free schools' policy would cause chaos for schools. It would destroy the vital central co-ordination of services for special needs children.'

Europe: 'The logic of the Tories' position is to pull out of Europe, putting more than three million jobs, dependent on the single market, at risk.'

■ The election timetable ■

A British government is elected for up to five years, unless it is defeated in Parliament on a major issue. The Prime Minister chooses the date of the next General Election, but does not have to wait until the end of the five years. A time is chosen which will give as much advantage as possible to the political party in power. Other politicians and the newspapers try very hard to guess which date the Prime Minister will choose.

About a month before the election the Prime Minister meets a small group of close advisers to discuss the date which would best suit the party.

The date is announced to the Cabinet. The Prime Minister formally asks the Sovereign to dissolve Parliament.

Once Parliament is dissolved, all MPs are unemployed, but government officers continue to function.

Party manifestos are published and campaigning begins throughout the country, lasting for about three weeks with large-scale press, radio and television coverage.

Voting takes place on Polling Day (usually a Thursday). The results from each constituency are announced as soon as the votes have been counted, usually the same night. The national result is known by the next morning at the latest.

As soon as it is clear that one party has a majority of seats in the House of Commons, its leader is formally invited by the Sovereign to form a government.

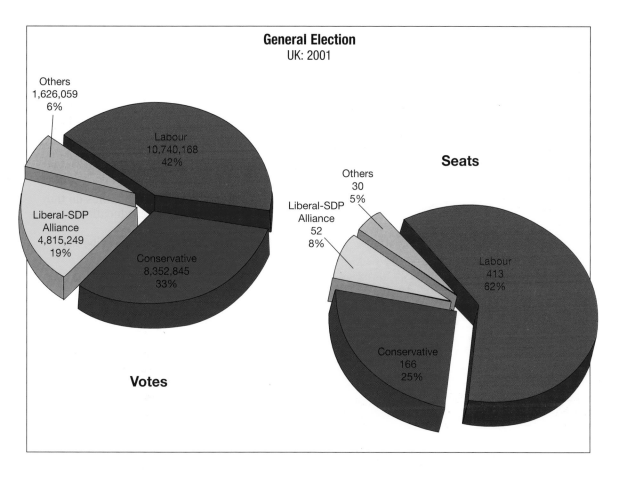

General Election
UK: 2001

Others
1,626,059
6%

Labour
10,740,168
42%

Liberal-SDP
Alliance
4,815,249
19%

Conservative
8,352,845
33%

Votes

Seats

Others
30
5%

Liberal-SDP
Alliance
52
8%

Labour
413
62%

Conservative
166
25%

Comprehension

Use the information on these two pages to answer the questions.

1 In 2001 which of the biggest British political parties supported the following policies?
  a local administration of schools
  b encouraging people to pay for private health care
  c allowing people out of prison early
  d not joining the European currency
  e cutting petrol prices
2 How is the date of a British general election decided?
3 What was the difference between the number of people who voted for the Alliance and the number of parliamentary seats they won?

Discussion

Work in pairs.

1 What advantages would a government have if it had a very large parliamentary majority?
2 Why do you think the Alliance got so few parliamentary seats?
3 If you were a British voter, which party do you think you would vote for and why?

■ A Member of Parliament ■

Dafydd Elis Thomas in his constituency

Introduction

Dafydd Elis Thomas was President of Plaid Cymru, the Party of Wales. He was one of three Welsh nationalist MPs who won seats at the 1987 General Election.

Meirionydd Nant Conwy (Gwynedd) E. 31,632	
D. E. Thomas, P.C.	10,392
D. T. Jones, C.	7,366
H. G. Roberts, Lab.	4,397
D. L. Roberts, S.D.P./All.	3,847
P.C. maj.	3,026

1 What was his majority at the 1987 General Election?
2 What parties did the other candidates represent?

Listening

1 Listen to Part 1 of the tape and answer the questions.
   a Which of these regions are mentioned: Brittany, Flanders, Latvia, Galicia, Lithuania, the Basque country, Estonia?
   b What are the titles of the government departments responsible for Wales and Scotland?
   c Which of these responsibilities do they have: health, defence, education, agriculture?
   d How does the speaker describe the Secretary of State for Wales?

2 Listen to Part 2 and answer the questions.
   a Which of these parties does Plaid Cymru work with in Parliament: Conservatives, Ulster Unionists, Labour, Scottish National Party, Social and Liberal Democrats?
   b Where do Plaid Cymru members sit in the House of Commons?
   c What sort of person might be a Privy Councillor?
   d Why isn't it safe to speak Welsh in the House of Commons?

3 Listen to the tape again and make brief notes about the kind of work the speaker does as an MP and about the problems he meets.

Discussion

Work in pairs.

1 In the speaker's view, what are the advantages of stronger regional government in Western Europe?
2 How do small parties operate in the House of Commons?

■ Summary ■

Vocabulary

1 Use these words and expressions from the unit to fill the gaps in the sentences below:
   constituencies   Opposition
   private sector   manifesto
   general election   devolution

   a The United Kingdom is divided into about 650 parliamentary . . . .
   b A . . . . takes place every four or five years.
   c Before an election, each party prepares a . . . . which outlines their policies.
   d An important Conservative policy was the return of state industries to the . . . .
   e The Labour government asked the public to vote on . . . . in Scotland and Wales.
   f While the Conservatives were in power, Labour formed the official . . . .

2 Work in pairs. Use the six expressions above to write sentences about your own political system.

Discussion

Work in pairs.

1 From your own knowledge, what effect did Margaret Thatcher and Tony Blair have in international affairs?
2 What is the United Kingdom's policy towards your own country and could it be improved?
3 How many of the political issues mentioned in this unit are important in your country? Which parties are for and against them? Are there other important political issues which have not been mentioned here?

Writing

1 In the interview, Dafydd Elis Thomas describes the kind of work he does as a Welsh MP. From your notes on the tape, list his examples. Write a short paragraph describing his work and its problems.
2 What are the equivalent of MPs in your own country? What does their work involve? List their responsibilities and write a short paragraph describing their work.

Voters at a polling station

The Law

■ The legal system ■

British law comes from two main sources: laws made in Parliament (usually drawn up by government departments and lawyers), and Common Law, which is based on previous judgements and customs. Just as there is no written constitution, so England and Wales have no criminal code or civil code and the interpretation of the law is based on what has happened in the past. The laws which are made in Parliament are interpreted by the courts, but changes in the law itself are made in Parliament.

The Central Criminal Court in London: the Old Bailey

The most common type of law court in England and Wales is the magistrates' court. There are 700 magistrates' courts and about 30,000 magistrates.

More serious criminal cases then go to the Crown Court, which has 90 branches in different towns and cities. Civil cases (for example, divorce or bankruptcy cases) are dealt with in County courts.

Appeals are heard by higher courts. For example, appeals from magistrates' courts are heard in the Crown Court, unless they are appeals on points of law. The highest court of appeal in England and Wales is the House of Lords. (Scotland has its own High Court in

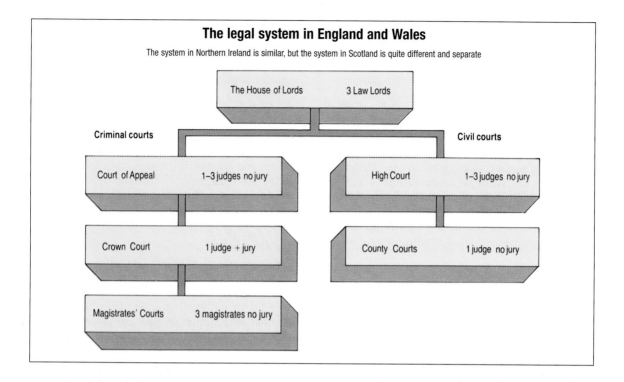

The legal system in England and Wales

The system in Northern Ireland is similar, but the system in Scotland is quite different and separate

The House of Lords | 3 Law Lords

Criminal courts

Court of Appeal | 1–3 judges no jury

Crown Court | 1 judge + jury

Magistrates' Courts | 3 magistrates no jury

Civil courts

High Court | 1–3 judges no jury

County Courts | 1 judge no jury

Edinburgh which hears all appeals from Scottish courts.) Certain cases may be referred to the European Court of Justice in Luxembourg. In addition, individuals have made the British Government change its practices in a number of areas as a result of petitions to the European Court of Human Rights.

The legal system also includes juvenile courts (which deal with offenders under seventeen) and coroners' courts (which investigate violent, sudden or unnatural deaths). There are administrative tribunals which make quick, cheap and fair decisions with much less formality. Tribunals deal with professional standards or disputes between individuals and government departments (for example, over taxation).

Criminal law is concerned with wrongful acts harmful to the community.

Civil law is concerned with individuals' rights, duties and obligations towards one another.

Comprehension

Use the information on these two pages to answer the questions.

1 Who is responsible for making laws in Britain?
2 In the United Kingdom, what is the difference between criminal and civil law?
3 What is the most common type of law court in England and Wales?
4 Name three other types of British courts.

Discussion

Work in pairs.

1 Why are some laws in Britain affected by laws outside Britain?
2 Which courts do you think would deal with the following:
   a a bank robbery?
   b a divorce case?
   c a burglary committed by a fifteen-year-old?
   d a drowning?
   e a case of driving too fast?

■ People in law cases ■

Solicitors

There are about 50,000 solicitors, a number which is rapidly increasing, and they make up by far the largest branch of the legal profession in England and Wales. They are found in every town, where they deal with all the day-to-day work of preparing legal documents for buying and selling houses, making wills, etc. Until the 1990s, only barristers represented clients in the higher courts. Today the situation is changing and solicitors may represent clients in a range of courts, in addition to preparing court cases for their clients and briefing barristers.

Barristers

There are about 5,000 barristers who defend or prosecute in the higher courts. Although solicitors and barristers work together on cases, barristers specialise in representing clients in court. While both types of lawyer take the Common Professional examination, thereafter their training and career structure are separate. In court, barristers wear wigs and gowns in keeping with the extreme formality of the proceedings. The highest level of barristers have the title QC (Queen's Counsel).

Judges

There are a few hundred judges, usually trained as barristers, who preside in more serious cases. There is no separate training for judges.

Jury

A jury consists of twelve people ('jurors'), who are ordinary people chosen at random from the Electoral Register (the list of people who can vote in elections). The jury listen to the evidence given in court in certain criminal cases and decide whether the defendant is guilty or innocent. If the person is found guilty, the punishment is passed by the presiding judge. Juries are rarely used in civil cases.

Magistrates

There are about 30,000 magistrates (Justices of the Peace, or JPs), who judge cases in the lower courts. They are usually unpaid and have no formal legal qualifications, but they are respectable people who are given some training.

Coroners

Coroners have medical or legal training (or both), and inquire into violent or unnatural deaths.

Clerks of the court

Clerks look after administrative and legal matters in the courtroom.

■ The police ■

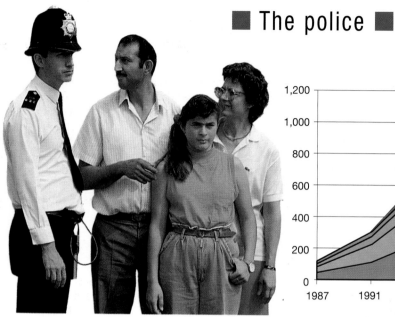

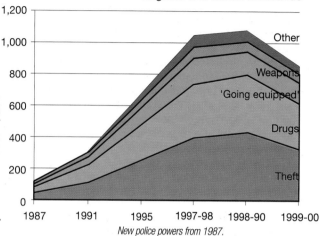

Police stop and search
England and Wales: thousands

New police powers from 1987.
'Going equipped' means carrying tools for burglary, etc.

Each of Britain's fifty-two police forces is responsible for law enforcement in its own area. In addition there are various national and regional connections (for example, in areas of training or the transfer of criminal records), and local forces cooperate with each other. Some special services, such as the Fraud Squad (who investigate financial crimes), are available to any local force in England and Wales. In general, however, the local police forces work independently under their own Chief Constables. Each force is maintained by a local police authority. The exception is London, where the Metropolitan Police are responsible to the Home Secretary.

Police duties cover a wide range of activities, from traffic control to more specialised departments such as river police. Each independent force has a uniformed branch and a Criminal Investigation Department (CID) with detectives in plain clothes. In addition the police authorities in England and Wales employ well over 50,000 civilians and over 3,000 traffic wardens.

Britain has relatively few police – approximately one policeman for every 400 people – and traditionally they are armed only with truncheons except in special circumstances. However, recent years have seen some major changes in police policy in response to industrial disputes and inner city violence in Great Britain. There has been an increase in the number of special units trained in crowd and riot control and in the use of firearms, a controversial area for the British police. The number of police has risen along with the crime rate. In recent years, they have become more accountable as a result of highly publicised cases of police corruption and racism.

Comprehension

Use the information on these two pages to answer the questions.

1 What is the difference between a solicitor and a barrister?
2 How are people chosen to serve on a jury?
3 Give three examples of basic police work.
4 Do police officers in Britain carry guns?
5 Is there a national police force in Britain?

Discussion

Work in pairs.

1 Can you identify the people in charge of the police in Britain?
2 Which do you think is better: judgement by one trained lawyer or judgement by twelve ordinary people?

■ Crime and punishment ■

Crime

About 90 per cent of all crimes are dealt with by magistrates' courts. Sentences (that is, the punishments decided by the court) vary a lot but most people who are found guilty have to pay a fine. Magistrates' courts can impose fines of up to £2,000 or prison sentences of up to six months. If the punishment is to be more severe the case must go to a Crown Court. The most severe punishment is life imprisonment: there has been no death penalty in Britain since 1965.

The level of recorded crime and the number of people sent to prison both rose rapidly during the last thirty years of the twentieth century. By 2001 the prison population had risen to over 64,000 and although it has fallen slightly since, there are serious concerns

Inside a prison

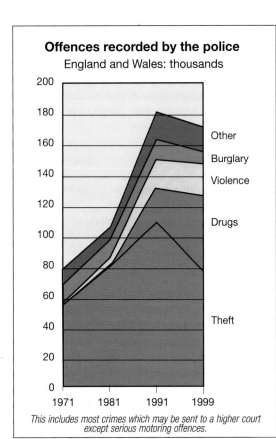

Offences recorded by the police
England and Wales: thousands

Other
Burglary
Violence
Drugs
Theft

This includes most crimes which may be sent to a higher court except serious motoring offences.

within the prison service about the numbers and conditions. The weekly cost of keeping someone in prison is higher than the average wage.

Punishment

These are some of the punishments available to judges.
Prison
Suspended sentences: the offender does not go to prison unless he or she commits another offence
Probation: normal life at home, but under supervision
Youth custody in special centres for young adults
Short disciplinary training in a detention centre
Community service: decorating old people's houses, etc.
Compensation: paying, or working for, one's victim
Fines: the punishment in 80 per cent of cases
Disqualification from driving
Fixed penalty fines: especially for parking offences

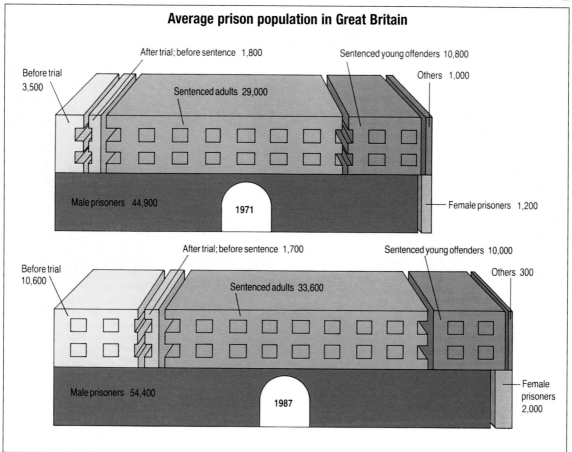

Average prison population in Great Britain

1971

Before trial 3,500
After trial; before sentence 1,800
Sentenced adults 29,000
Sentenced young offenders 10,800
Others 1,000
Male prisoners 44,900
Female prisoners 1,200

1987

Before trial 10,600
After trial; before sentence 1,700
Sentenced adults 33,600
Sentenced young offenders 10,000
Others 300
Male prisoners 54,400
Female prisoners 2,000

Comprehension

Use the information on these two pages to answer the questions.

1 What are the most common offences in England and Wales?
2 What is the most common form of punishment?
3 Which crimes have increased most in recent years?
4 Describe the following:
   a The difference between the numbers of male and female prisoners in British prisons.
   b Changes in the total number of prisoners.

Discussion

Work in pairs.

1 Which punishment do you think is suitable for each of the following crimes?
   a murder of a policeman
   b vandalising a telephone box
   c drinking and driving, without causing an accident
   d robbing a supermarket with a gun
   e stealing goods from a shop ('shoplifting')
   f parking a car illegally

2 Match these actual sentences from British courts with the crimes in Question 1.
   a five to ten years in prison
   b a small fixed penalty fine
   c life imprisonment
   d a £400 fine
   e a £200 fine and disqualification from driving
   f 100 hours of community service

■ A solicitor's work ■

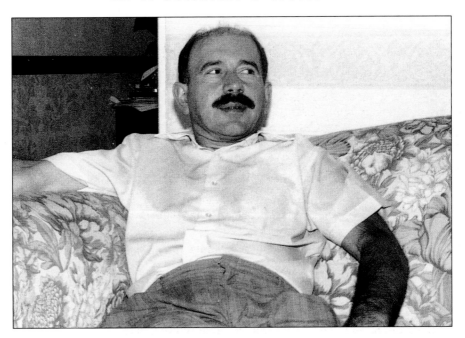

Introduction

In England and Wales, before you can take the professional examinations to become a solicitor, you have to be one of the following:

a a law graduate with a university degree in law

b a non-graduate with a degree in any other subject

c a non-graduate with practical experience in a law firm.

The professional examinations are run by the Law Society.

1 What is a solicitor?

2 Which of these professions do you think has the lowest pay: solicitors, doctors, dentists, surveyors, accountants?

Listening

As you listen to the tape, make brief notes to help you answer the following questions:

1 When did the speaker leave university?

2 Which of the following are true now, true when the speaker left university or both? Write *now*, *then* or *both*.

a Non-law graduates must have legal training.

b Local authorities pay for legal training.

c Big law firms pay for legal training.

d It is called the Common Professional Examination.

3 In the speaker's opinion, which of the professions in the *Introduction* has the lowest pay?

4 Why does he think this is so?

5 What did one of his clients do with a letter he received at 4.30 p.m.?

6 Why is Monday morning particularly busy?

Discussion

Work in pairs.

1 What evidence is there in the tape that solicitors are overworked and underpaid?

2 What do you think the clients' view would be?

■ Summary ■

Vocabulary

1 The law has its own vocabulary. Match these words from the unit with their definitions.

a	arrest	person charged in a court of law
b	bankruptcy	give a punishment
c	burglary	found to have broken a law
d	defendant	stick carried by a policeman
e	fraud	inability to pay one's debts
f	guilty	breaking into a building to steal
g	prosecute	deceiving to make money
h	sentence	seize a person by law
i	statute	law established by Parliament
j	truncheon	bring a criminal charge against someone

2 Define the following words:

vandalism   magistrate   firearm   tribunal   juvenile   jury

Discussion

1 The average prison population in England and Wales has risen almost every year since the Second World War. One possible solution is to continue building new prisons. Is this the only possibility?

2 In Britain, the average salary of an eighteen-year-old trainee police officer is about 30 per cent higher than for a newly qualified teacher. Should police officers be paid more than teachers?

3 'During the last decade or so there have been disturbing changes in British policing . . . Once the police have appropriate training and equipment, those in authority seem prepared to use them rather than find political solutions to problems' (*State of the Nation*).

What is meant by 'appropriate training and equipment'? How will these changes affect the image of the traditional British policeman?

Writing

Use the notes you made on the interview on the opposite page to write a short paragraph on the work of a solicitor in England.

6

Britain and the World

■ The Commonwealth ■

The Queen with Commonwealth Prime Ministers

In 1920 the British Empire controlled a fifth of the world's land surface. Today the Empire has developed into a voluntary association of over fifty independent states with a combined population of more than a quarter of the world's people, including some of the richest countries and some of the poorest.

This voluntary association of nations began when Britain's older colonies (Australia, Canada, New Zealand and South Africa) became independent nations. The dismantling of the Empire has been a gradual process: right up until 1962 the citizens of this huge area had the automatic right to live and work in Britain itself. This is no longer the case.

Today Britain has only fourteen 'dependent territories', which rely on Britain for their defence. All of these are tiny (except the British Antarctic Territory, which is uninhabited). When Hong Kong was returned to China in 1997, the remaining territories had a population of less than 200,000.

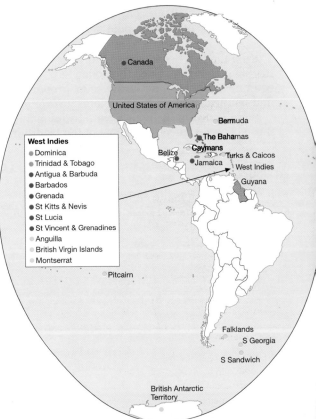

The Queen is Head of the Commonwealth. She is also recognised as Head of State in eighteen countries, including Canada and Australia. Although Britain maintains a strong influence in the Commonwealth, and the Queen takes a keen personal interest in Commonwealth matters, despite her title she has little real power.

The modern Commonwealth includes republics and other monarchies in addition to states headed by the Queen. In 1950 India became a republic while remaining within the Commonwealth. Since then most of Britain's former dependent territories have become independent and have remained within the Commonwealth. Mozambique, a former Portuguese colony, is the only Commonwealth member with no previous British connection.

Comprehension

Use the information on these two pages to answer the questions.

1 How many countries are there in the Commonwealth?
2 Which parts of the world have the most Commonwealth countries?
3 Give an example of each of the following:
   a a dependent territory
   b a country where the Queen is Head of State
   c a country which has left the Commonwealth.
4 Is Hong Kong still a British colony?

Discussion

Work in pairs.

1 What differences can you discover between the Commonwealth in 1920 and the Commonwealth today?
2 Can you see any advantages in being a member of the Commonwealth?

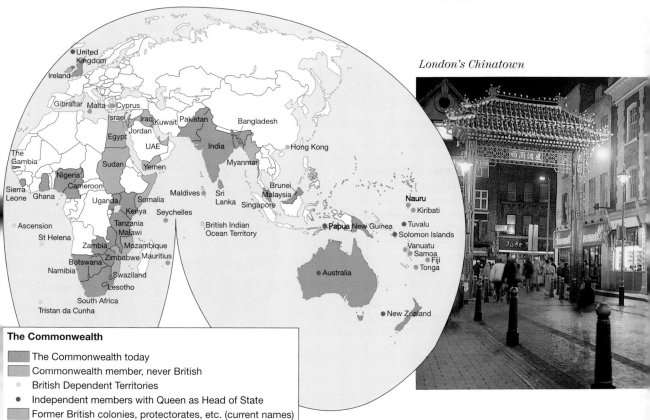

London's Chinatown

The Commonwealth

- The Commonwealth today
- Commonwealth member, never British
- British Dependent Territories
- Independent members with Queen as Head of State
- Former British colonies, protectorates, etc. (current names)

Map labels: United Kingdom, Ireland, Gibraltar, Malta, Cyprus, Israel, Iraq, Kuwait, Pakistan, Bangladesh, Jordan, Egypt, UAE, India, Hong Kong, The Gambia, Sudan, Yemen, Myanmar, Nigeria, Cameroon, Sierra Leone, Ghana, Uganda, Somalia, Maldives, Sri Lanka, Brunei, Malaysia, Singapore, Nauru, Kiribati, Ascension, Kenya, Seychelles, British Indian Ocean Territory, Papua New Guinea, Tuvalu, Solomon Islands, St Helena, Tanzania, Malawi, Vanuatu, Samoa, Zambia, Mozambique, Fiji, Botswana, Zimbabwe, Mauritius, Tonga, Namibia, Swaziland, Lesotho, Australia, South Africa, Tristan da Cunha, New Zealand

■ Multicultural Britain ■

Immediately after the Second World War, Britain looked like a prosperous and friendly country for an immigrant worker. All Commonwealth citizens were free to enter the country and look for work, which was plentiful. However, since the Immigration Act of 1962, successive governments have introduced regulations to restrict the number of immigrants.

It is difficult to get statistics on race, but the following patterns are clear. The percentage of non-whites in Britain increased quite rapidly between 1945 and the end of the 1970s and the 2001 Census will show that it had reached 10 per cent by then. In addition, the number of people seeking political asylum reached 70,000 a year in 2001.

Ethnic minorities are concentrated in the cities. The percentage of members of ethnic minorities who are unemployed, or in low-grade jobs, is higher than in the population as a whole.

Racial discrimination and poor living conditions have contributed to racial violence, especially in the day-to-day form of relations between young blacks and the police, or in the more extreme form of inner-city riots. This is despite the Race Relations Act (1976), which was designed to promote equality of opportunity for people of all races.

Immigrants permitted to settle
UK: thousands
Asia   Other

1976   1986   1996   1999

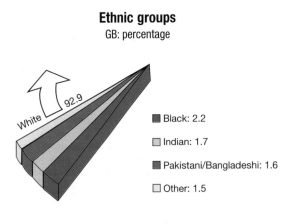

Ethnic groups
GB: percentage

White 92.9

■ Black: 2.2
□ Indian: 1.7
■ Pakistani/Bangladeshi: 1.6
□ Other: 1.5

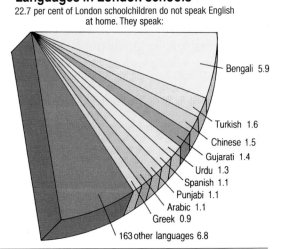

Languages in London schools
22.7 per cent of London schoolchildren do not speak English at home. They speak:

Bengali 5.9
Turkish 1.6
Chinese 1.5
Gujarati 1.4
Urdu 1.3
Spanish 1.1
Punjabi 1.1
Arabic 1.1
Greek 0.9
163 other languages 6.8

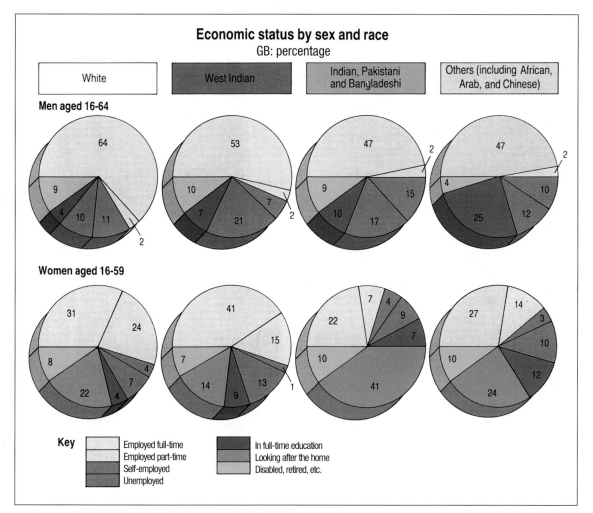

Economic status by sex and race
GB: percentage

| White | West Indian | Indian, Pakistani and Bangladeshi | Others (including African, Arab, and Chinese) |

Men aged 16-64

White: 64, 9, 4, 10, 11, 2
West Indian: 53, 10, 7, 21, 7, 2
Indian, Pakistani and Bangladeshi: 47, 2, 9, 15, 10, 17
Others: 47, 2, 4, 10, 12, 25

Women aged 16-59

White: 31, 24, 8, 22, 4, 7, 4
West Indian: 41, 15, 7, 13, 1, 9, 14
Indian, Pakistani and Bangladeshi: 7, 4, 9, 7, 22, 10, 41
Others: 14, 3, 10, 12, 24, 10, 27

Key
- Employed full-time
- Employed part-time
- Self-employed
- Unemployed
- In full-time education
- Looking after the home
- Disabled, retired, etc.

■ Religion in a multi-ethnic society ■

'Dei Gratia Regina, Fidei Defensor' still appears abbreviated on British coins: 'By the Grace of God Queen, Defender of the Faith'. The Queen is head of the Church of England, but is Britain a Christian country? Although many people say they are Christians, this is not reflected in church membership, which is only 13 per cent of the population in England. It is much higher (80 per cent) in Northern Ireland, but there religion is part of deep social divisions. Membership of the larger Christian denominations is falling, while the membership of other religions is rising.

The main religious groups
Christian

Anglicans: nearly a third of the population say they are members of the Church of England, the Protestant state church, but only about one million go to services each Sunday.

Catholics: members of the Roman Catholic church, about 10 per cent of the population.

Nonconformists: members of other Protestant churches such as Baptists, Methodists and Presbyterians (the state church of Scotland).

Pentecostalists: mainly in the West Indian community.

Anglican parish church

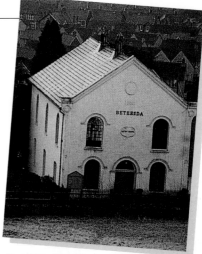

Baptist chapel

Muslim mosque

Jewish synagogue

Sikh temple

Non-Christian

Muslims: now represent about 2 per cent of the population.

Hindus: currently about 1 per cent of the population.

Jews: the second largest Jewish community in Europe.

Sikhs: strongly represented, as are Buddhists and other non-Christian religions.

No religion: nearly half the population of Great Britain say they have no religion, particularly younger people.

Comprehension

Use the information on pages 46 to 48 to answer the questions.

1 What proportion of the British population is non-white, and where do their families come from?
2 Where do most non-whites live in Britain?
3 What is the state religion in Britain?
4 What other religions are represented?

Discussion

Work in pairs.

1 Which ethnic groups have the largest percentage of:
   a self-employed?   c housewives?
   b unemployed?   d students?
   Describe any other contrasts between the economic status of men and women in different ethnic groups.
2 What evidence can you find that Britain is no longer a Christian country?

■ Britain and Europe ■

The European Union

Britain joined the European Community in 1973 under a Conservative government. Britain was the sixth country to join (a number of other countries have done so since) and membership was to be 'of unlimited duration'. This was in accord with the terms of the original Treaty of Rome, which started the Community in 1958. In 1975 Parliament's decision that Britain should become a member was confirmed by a referendum of the whole electorate (the first in British history): over eight million wanted to get out, but over seventeen million wanted to stay in. Therefore Britain continued to be a member, although not all the members of the Labour government which called the referendum were sure that this was the right decision.

Britain's membership has not always been easy. There have been arguments over financial and agricultural policies, and for many people the way the European Union operates remains a mystery. On the other hand, Britain's poorer regions have benefited, receiving 24 per cent of the Union's regional and social funds in 1985, for example. Overall, however, Britain is a major net contributor to the Union's funds. Nearly half of Britain's trade is with the rest of the European Union.

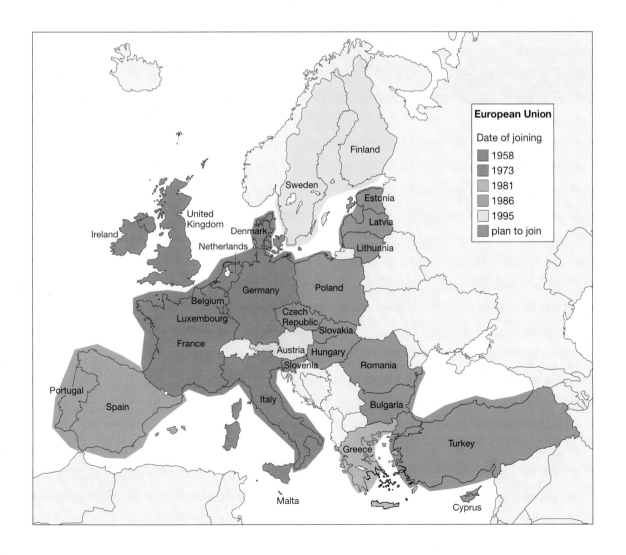

European Union

Date of joining
- 1958
- 1973
- 1981
- 1986
- 1995
- plan to join

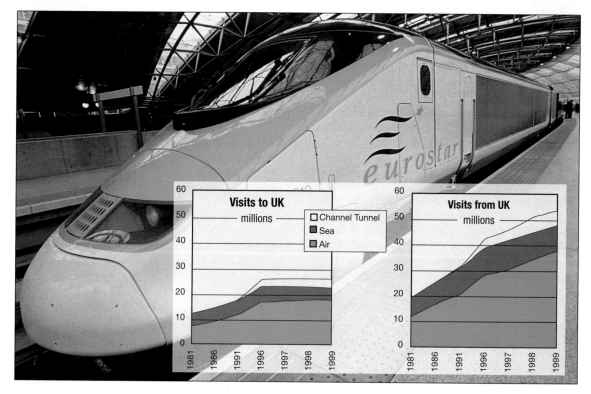

(above left) *Eurostar train*

Closer to Europe

Over the last 200 years the idea of a tunnel under the sea between Britain and France has been put forward a number of times. On several occasions, construction has actually been started: one project was abandoned as recently as 1975. In 1987 a new Anglo-French group called Eurotunnel was chosen to construct a system which would link the road and rail networks of Britain and France and improve communications and commercial links inside the European Union. The Channel Tunnel has been fully operational since 1995. Within three years it accounted for 12 per cent of all traffic to and from the United Kingdom. There are two rail tunnels and a service tunnel, each nearly 50 kilometres long. There is also a possibility that a separate road tunnel for cars and lorries will be built in the future.

(above right) *French and British workers celebrating the linking of the Channel Tunnel* (centre) *Working in the tunnel* (right) *The Channel Tunnel route*

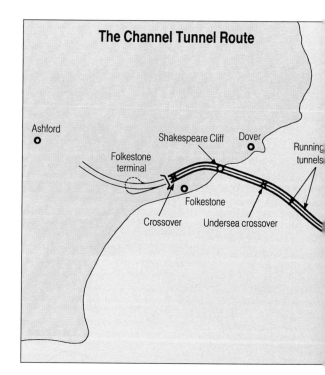

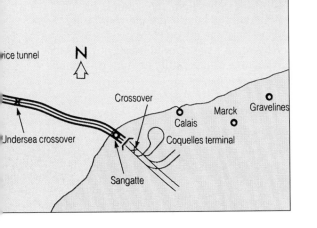

Comprehension

Use the information on pages 49 to 51 to answer the questions.

1 When did Britain hold its first referendum and what was the result?
2 How many countries are there in the European Union?
3 Is the idea of a Channel Tunnel a new one?
4 How much is the Channel Tunnel used?

Discussion

Work in pairs.

1 From your own information and the information on these pages, what reasons can you find for, and against, continued British membership of the European Union?
2 'If the Channel Tunnel is really necessary, why hasn't it been built before?' Give your own opinions.

■ Race relations ■

Introduction

The speaker was born in Guyana in South America. Her family are originally from India. She has lived in south-east England since early childhood. She is married to a solicitor.

1 What do you think she does for a living?
  a She's a housewife, with small children (toddlers).
  b She runs her own business, selling balloons for special occasions.
  c She works as a legal secretary in her husband's firm.
  d She runs an aerobics class in a town called Thame.

2 Before listening, try to reconstruct her two experiences, (a) and (b), from these words on the tape:
  a toddler group   coloured   wary   threatened   popular
  b balloon   christening   lunchtime   currant bun   strict Muslim   leg of pork

Listening

1 What is Thame like?
2 Do many people from ethnic minorities live there?
3 How did other Thame people react to her:
  a when they first met her?
  b when they got to know her?
4 Why does she think she's popular?
5 What sort of family did she visit? Why?
6 What was she offered?
7 Why wasn't she offered ham?
8 What was she actually having for lunch?

Discussion

Work in pairs.

1 Why do you think people were surprised to meet the speaker, after hearing her on the telephone?
2 How would you summarise her experience in a small English town?

■ Summary ■

Vocabulary

1 Put three of the following words under each of these headings:
The Commonwealth; Immigration; Religion; Europe.

   agricultural policy Anglican colony
   discrimination empire minority
   multi-ethnic Nonconformist Protestant
   referendum territory treaty

2 Make pairs of opposites out of the following list of words.

   compulsory criticise emigration
   former gradual huge immigration
   national poorest praise present
   regional richest sudden tiny
   voluntary

Discussion

1 How has Britain's colonial past affected Britain today?
2 In what ways has Britain become more multicultural? What problems have arisen as a result? Are there similar problems in your own country?
3 From your own experience, who do you think benefits most from a united Europe?

Writing

1 Collect information on the following topics.
   a Britain's past connections with the rest of the world.
   b Britain's future connections with the rest of the world.
2 Organise your information into two paragraphs and write an account of Britain's international relations.

Energy and the Environment

■ Environmental issues ■

Although Britain is densely populated, it still has large areas of open countryside, including National Parks, Areas of Outstanding Natural Beauty and Royal Parks. Many special sites are protected because they are of architectural or historical value (for example, see Stonehenge above). In addition to the Government's Department of the Environment there are a number of voluntary organisations which are involved in protecting buildings and the countryside.

Over the last twenty years there have been changes in patterns of agriculture and urban development. Traditional heavy industries such as iron and steel have declined and inner-city areas have declined with them. At the same time, new towns have been built and the pressure on the countryside from roads and houses has increased. People have moved away from the big cities and there has been a battle to keep parts of the 'Green Belt' from development.

Changes in agriculture have meant bigger farms with bigger fields, with less room for plants and wildlife in hedges, and an increased danger of soil erosion in some areas. Mineral workings, intensive forestry and the use of nitrates in fertilisers, as well as the general increase in the amount of pesticides, have created concern for the future.

In some ways, Britain is a less polluted country than it was thirty years ago. Coal burning is strictly controlled in areas like London, which no longer suffers the poisonous smogs that killed people in the 1950s. Attempts have been made to landscape areas of wasteland, to repair and restore the old canals and to clean up Britain's rivers. But despite these efforts various serious threats to the environment remain: acid rain caused partly by sulphur emissions from power stations, the rise in the number of cars and lorries on the roads, the pollution of the sea, the destruction of old buildings and the spread of housing. There is continuing debate on the safety of nuclear power and the possibility of alternative sources of energy.

Protected land
England and Wales

3,442 Sites of Special Scientific Interest 6% of land

14 Green Belts 10% of land

36 Areas of Outstanding Natural Beauty 11% of land

10 National Parks 10% of land

Conservation and threat

Dounreay

Loch Torridon

Glen Affric

Cairngorm

Glen Nevis and Glencoe

Trossachs

Northumberland

Galloway

Hartlepool

Antrim

Sperrin

Lake District

Sellafield

Fermanagh

Yorkshire Dales

North York Moors

Mourne

Lincolnshire Wolds

Snowdonia

Peak District

Shropshire Hills

Sizewell

Brecon Beacons

Cotswolds

Chilterns

Bradwell

Exmoor

Sussex Downs

Dungeness

Dartmoor

Winfrith

Key

- Coastal conservation zones
- National Parks and Areas of Outstanding Natural Beauty
- 'Green belts' around cities
- Severely polluted areas
- Untreated sewage discharge
- ■ Nuclear power stations and reprocessing plants sending radionuclides into the sea
- Acid rain areas (over 0.04g of hydrogen ions per m²)

Comprehension

Use the information on these two pages to answer the questions.

1 Are most National Parks found in highland or lowland areas? Name four of them.
2 How much of the land in England and Wales is protected? Who is responsible for protecting the environment? What examples of protection are given?
3 How has agriculture in Britain changed?
4 What has happened to the London smogs and why?

Discussion

Work in pairs.

1 List four things which threaten the environment and suggest what can be done about them.
2 Which parts of your own country are most in need of protection: cities or the countryside? Give reasons for your decision.

■ Looking after the environment ■

The area covered by forest and woodland more than doubled in the twentieth century and now covers over ten per cent of Britain, 2 per cent more than in 1989. The state-run Forestry Commission monitors the health and sustainability of its forests.

In many parts of upland Britain the Forestry Commission planted dense squares of evergreen trees which did not fit in with the irregular native woods, but modern state-run forests are planted with more thought for their effect on the environment.

Durdle Door, Dorset

North Sea pollution

The National Trust was set up in 1895. It is a voluntary society with a million and a half members and it now owns more than 200,000 hectares, particularly in the Lake District and North Wales. It has 190 houses open to the public, 51 villages, 38 pubs and nearly 12,000 farms. Durdle Door, on the Dorset Coastal Path, is part of its Enterprise Neptune scheme, which protects 800 km of coast.

The North Sea is in danger of becoming poisoned to death. More than 70 million tonnes of industrial waste are dumped into it each year. If river pollution is included, at least 50,000 different chemicals get into the North Sea, including heavy metals like mercury, lead and arsenic, highly poisonous chlorinated compounds and fertilisers which can kill fish and make shellfish unsafe to eat.

Until the 1960s, mining waste in the coalfields was left on the surface in ugly heaps. These are now landscaped and grassed over to provide a safer and cleaner environment.

The disposal of nuclear and other dangerous waste continues to be a problem as available land decreases. It is estimated that an area of countryside the size of London disappears into urban, industrial and recreational use every twelve years.

Trees affected by acid rain

The United Kingdom is responsible for 2 per cent of the man-made carbon dioxide in the earth's atmosphere. Unlike most European countries, it has managed to reduce emissions of this greenhouse gas, which contributes to global warming, but Germany has been much more successful in doing so. The goal is to cut carbon dioxide emissions to 80 per cent of the 1990 level by the year 2010. The United Kingdom is also committed to the United Nations Kyoto Protocol signed in 1997. It must reduce emissions of six greenhouse gases to 87.5 per cent of the 1990 level by the year 2012.

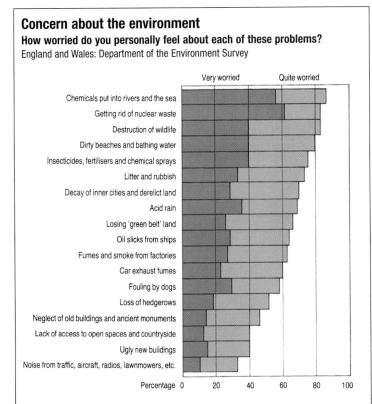

Concern about the environment
How worried do you personally feel about each of these problems?
England and Wales: Department of the Environment Survey

Very worried   Quite worried

- Chemicals put into rivers and the sea
- Getting rid of nuclear waste
- Destruction of wildlife
- Dirty beaches and bathing water
- Insecticides, fertilisers and chemical sprays
- Litter and rubbish
- Decay of inner cities and derelict land
- Acid rain
- Losing 'green belt' land
- Oil slicks from ships
- Fumes and smoke from factories
- Car exhaust fumes
- Fouling by dogs
- Loss of hedgerows
- Neglect of old buildings and ancient monuments
- Lack of access to open spaces and countryside
- Ugly new buildings
- Noise from traffic, aircraft, radios, lawnmowers, etc.

Percentage 0   20   40   60   80   100

Comprehension

Use the information on these two pages to answer the questions.

1 Which pictures illustrate threats to the environment?
2 Which pictures illustrate improvements to the environment?
3 Which of the concerns in the questionnaire are not illustrated or mentioned in the text?
4 List the five threats to the environment which people are most worried about, according to the questionnaire.

Discussion

Work in pairs.

1 Make your own questionnaire on the environment.
2 Collect the opinions of the rest of the class and report on your findings.

■ Britain's energy ■

Britain has the largest energy resources of any country in the European Union and is a major producer of oil, natural gas and coal. Other primary sources of energy are nuclear power and, to a lesser extent, water power.

Before the 1970s Britain depended on imports of oil from abroad but the discovery of large oil and gas reserves in the North Sea changed this dramatically: by 1986 about 2.2 million barrels of oil were extracted per day, making Britain the world's fifth largest producer. There are over thirty offshore oilfields from which oil and gas are piped to the mainland. Natural gas has replaced coal gas in the public supply system.

Britain has large reserves of coal, and coal mining played a very important part in the industrial revolution of the eighteenth and nineteenth centuries. By 1913 the coal industry employed over a million workers. Coal is still an important source of heat for both private houses and power stations, but in recent years the industry has greatly reduced the numbers of mines and miners while increasing efficiency. There was a long and bitter industrial dispute in 1984–85 as miners reacted to the beginning of this new phase in the development of the coal industry.

A coal mine

Nuclear power

'The government believes that nuclear power has a vital role in helping to meet Britain's long-term energy requirements.' (Central Office of Information)

'We are in favour of a balanced energy programme for our country's future. Nuclear electricity is not the only answer – but it is a clean, reliable, economic piece of the electricity jigsaw.' (Nuclear Energy Information Group)

'Studies from many countries indicate that all radioactive wastes can be managed and disposed of without undue risk to man or the environment.' (UK Atomic Energy Authority)

'Nuclear power is unsafe . . . and there is a long history of leaks and accidents.' (*State of the Nation*)

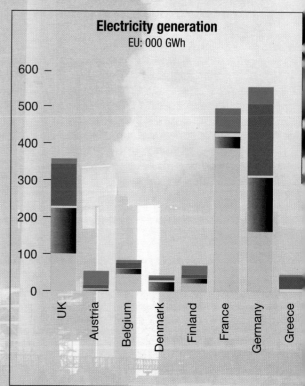

Electricity generation
EU: 000 GWh

'An accident on the scale of Chernobyl could happen here at any time.' (Greenpeace)

'We had to destroy sheep for two years after Chernobyl – here and in the Lake District. How do they know it was Chernobyl? We've got nuclear reactors on our doorsteps, and the radiation had never been measured before.' (A North Wales farmer)

Britain has fourteen nuclear power stations in operation. There are other nuclear installations too, such as reprocessing units and research centres. Since the original power stations started operations in 1956 there has been much discussion over the best design; pressurised water reactors are planned for the future and the government's eventual aim is to have 20 per cent of Britain's electricity produced by nuclear power.

All proposals for new power stations meet with public opposition, and this has increased since the disaster at Chernobyl in the Ukraine in 1986. There are fears that the reactors themselves are unsafe, and that the problems of waste disposal have not been solved. While those in favour of nuclear power claim that it is clean, safe and efficient, opponents argue that the dangers are too great and that other sources of energy have not been sufficiently researched because of lack of government funding or interest. The privatisation of the electricity industry has also raised the question of who should own and operate nuclear power stations.

Comprehension

Use the information on these two pages to answer the questions.

1 What are the major sources of energy in Britain?
2 How important is North Sea oil to Britain?
3 What do the quotations tell you about the government's viewpoint and other views of nuclear power?
4 Why is there opposition to the use of nuclear power?

Discussion

Work in pairs.

1 What similarities and differences are there between Britain's energy sources and those of your own country?
2 What are the most common forms of energy in your own country for home heating, cooking and the production of electricity?

A North Sea oil rig

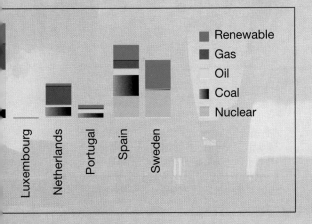

Renewable
Gas
Oil
Coal
Nuclear

Luxembourg Netherlands Portugal Spain Sweden

■ Greenhouse v green house ■

Introduction

1 What can you do in your own home to reduce damage to the global environment?
2 List five household goods which you would classify as 'green', and describe how buying them would help the environment.
3 List three things which could be recycled and used for further manufacture after you have used them.

Listening

1 Which green items does the speaker mention?
2 Why has she changed to green items only gradually?
3 Why does the speaker think that simply buying more expensive goods can help the environment?

4 When did green issues become news in Britain?
5 In the speaker's opinion, why have supermarkets started selling green goods?
6 What materials does the speaker recycle?
7 How does Sheffield City Council help the environment?
8 What particular problems might there be in doing the same in Brighton?

Discussion

Work in pairs.

1 From the evidence on the tape, how does Britain compare with your own country in developing green goods and services?
2 Can you think of any other ways in which households can help the environment?

■ Summary ■

Vocabulary

1 Divide these words and expressions from the unit into two lists: protectors of the environment; threats to the environment.
   power station wildlife landscaping hedge car erosion waste disposal lorry National Park fertiliser green belt sulphur emission intensive forestry urban development smog National Trust countryside pesticide Greenpeace acid rain

2 Discuss your list with another student and explain your choices.

Discussion

1 In your opinion, what are the greatest threats to the environment in Britain?
2 Are these threats present in your own country? Which areas of your own country have the worst pollution problems?
3 What are your own views on nuclear energy?
4 What do you think about the possibility of using other forms of energy, which are not harmful to the environment?

Writing

1 Make notes on the possible sources of pollution which worry you in your own area.
2 Write a letter to your local representative, or the company concerned, complaining about one of the sources of pollution you have noted and suggesting how it could be cleaned up.

A spoil heap, the waste products of coal mining, at Polkemmet Colliery, Scotland

8

Education

A traditional 'public' school

A modern primary school

▨ The school system ▨

Education is compulsory from the age of five to sixteen, and there is usually a move from primary to secondary school at about the age of eleven, but schools are organised in a number of different ways. The Department for Education and Skills maintains overall control although local education authorities and head teachers have considerable powers in planning and administration. The National Curriculum introduced in 1988 sets levels of attainment for all pupils at the end of Key Stages 1 – 3 at ages 7, 11 and 14.

Until the 1960s most children took an examination at the end of primary school (the Eleven Plus): those who passed went to grammar schools while those who did not went to secondary modern schools. A few areas still select at the age of eleven, but about 90 per cent of secondary schools in Britain are now comprehensive, taking children of all abilities from their local area.

Most parents choose to send their children to free state schools financed from public funds but an increasing number of secondary pupils attend fee-paying independent schools outside the state system. Many of these are boarding schools, which provide accommodation for pupils during term time. Many independent boarding schools are confusingly called public schools in England and Wales. Schools in Britain have three terms a year, each with a short half-term break in the middle, and longer holidays at Christmas and Easter and in the summer.

The school system in England and Wales
(The systems in Scotland and N Ireland are very different)

Sixth form: ages 16–18 (voluntary)

75% of pupils now continue in full-time education after the end of compulsory schooling at age 16. Only 45% did so in the 1980s.
They may study for **'A' levels** or **vocational** qualifications at:
    the **sixth form** of their own secondary school (state or private)
    a separate **sixth form college** or
    a **college of further education**

Advanced Level	Vocational
The usual requirement for university entrance. **24%** of women **20%** of men got two 'A' levels or more in 1999 (15% in 1989).	National targets are set for NVQs: national vocational qualifications. **75%** of 19-year-olds reached Level 2 in 2000 (target 85%).

Secondary school: ages 11–16 (compulsory)

8%

85% of 11–16 year-olds go to **comprehensive** schools, which do not select pupils by ability.
8% go to independent fee-paying schools which are also known as **public** schools.
Some areas still have a selection test at age eleven, called the **Eleven Plus**:
5% who pass go to **grammar** schools
2% who fail go to **secondary modern** schools
and the rest to comprehensive schools.

2% 5%

GCSE
51% of girls and **42%** of boys got 5 or more grade C results or higher in the General Certificate of Secondary Education in 1998.

Primary school: ages 5–11 (compulsory)

5%

95% of 5–11 year-olds go to state-funded **primary** schools, many of which are still run by churches. Like secondary school students they follow a **National Curriculum** with standardised tests at **key stages** every two years.

5% go to independent fee-paying schools. Some of these are called **preparatory** (or 'prep') schools. Here pupils may take the Common Entrance Examination set by the independent secondary schools.

Key Stages: KS
The National Curriculum has tests at primary school: **KS 1** age 5-7 **KS2** age 7-11 and secondary: **KS3** age 11-14 **KS4** age 14-16.

Pre-school: age 3–5 (voluntary)

64% of 3 and 4-year olds in the UK attend some form of **pre-school** education, compared with only 21% in 1970.
16% of 4-year olds in England attend some form of non-school education such as **playgroups** in the private and voluntary sector.

97% of 4-year olds in England have a free, part-time early education place. All 4-year olds in England and Wales are entitled to such a place if their parents wish. This will be extended to 3-year olds by 2004.

Foundation stage
The increasing emphasis on pre-school education means that children's skills will be assessed earlier and earlier.

Comprehension

Use the information on pages 62 and 63 to answer the questions.

1 At what age do pupils usually move from primary to secondary education?
2 What is the difference between selective and comprehensive education?
3 What percentage of secondary school children go to fee-paying schools?
4 Define the following: nursery school, boarding school, grammar school.

Discussion

Work in pairs.

1 Apart from the state, who else runs schools in Britain?
2 Describe you own education in terms which would make sense to someone familiar with the British system. You may have to use explanations like 'a kind of grammar school' or 'an upper secondary school'.

■ Politics and education ■

Changes in educational policy in Britain have frequently been the result of political decisions or changes of government. For example, the Labour government which came to power in 1964 immediately encouraged the spread of comprehensive schools and the abolition of selection at eleven. In the 1980s and 1990s the Conservatives made radical changes throughout the education system. Labour continued to change parts of the system from 1997 onwards.

SCHOOLS IN 1988

a State schools controlled by local authorities.
b Local authorities decide school budgets, including books, teachers' salaries, and cleaning.
c Children go to the school whose 'catchment area' they live in. This is usually, but not always, the nearest school to their home.
d All pupils study religion (the only subject required by law).
e Schools assess children's progress by their own internal tests.

CONSERVATIVE GOVERNMENT CHANGES

a Primary school children study English (and Welsh in Wales), maths, science, history, geography, art, music and physical education. Secondary-school pupils study a modern language up to the age of sixteen in addition.
b Parents choose the school their children go to.
c All children assessed by national tests at the ages of seven, eleven, fourteen and sixteen.
d Each school responsible for own budget, deciding whether to spend it on books, salaries or other services.
e Parents vote on whether to make their school independent of local authority control and receive money from central government.

A seven-year-old pupil studying for her assessment test (right) *Primary school children in an art class*

SCHOOLS IN 2001

a All schools are inspected by the Office for Standards in Education (Ofsted).
b Results of inspections are publicly available and are used by parents to choose their children's school.
c Schools follow a national curriculum including compulsory literacy and numeracy lessons.
d All children are tested at 'Key Stages' (see pages 62-63) by Standard Assessment Tests (SATS).

Comprehension

Use the information on these two pages to answer the questions.

1 Define the following:
      abolition   assessment   catchment area   local authority
2 Which subjects in the British National Curriculum have you studied in your own school system?
3 Match each government change with a feature of schools in 1988.
4 Find the outcome in 2001 which resulted from each of the government changes.

Discussion

Work in pairs.

1 Which of the changes do you think are improvements?
2 Which situation is most like the schools in your own country, 1988 or now?

■ After sixteen ■

Since 1988, most sixteen-year-olds have taken the General Certificate of Secondary Education (GCSE) or the Scottish Certificate of Education (SCE) in five, ten or even fifteen subjects.

Pupils going on to higher education or professional training usually take 'A' level examinations in two or three subjects. These require two more years of study after GCSE, either in the sixth form of a secondary school, or in a separate sixth-form college. Other pupils may choose vocational subjects such as catering, tourism, secretarial or building skills. Subsidised courses in these subjects are run at colleges of further education.

School-leavers with jobs sometimes take part-time vocational courses, on day-release from work. Colleges of further education and some schools offer vocational courses leading to national vocational qualifications (NVQs) as well as 'A' level courses.

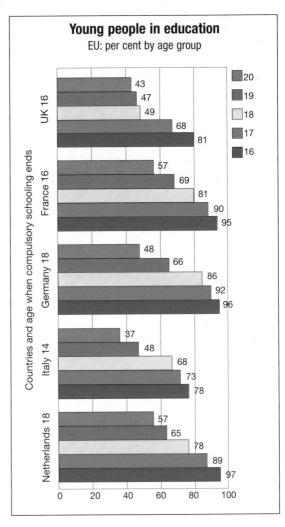

Young people in education
EU: per cent by age group

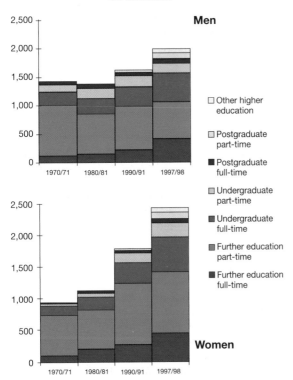

Students in further and higher education
UK: thousands

Higher education

There are over 100 universities in Britain plus other institutions including teacher training colleges.

Undergraduate courses normally take three years of full-time study, although a number of subjects take longer, including medicine, architecture and foreign languages (where courses may include a year abroad). They lead in most cases to a Bachelor's degree in Arts or Science. There are various postgraduate degrees, including Master of Philosophy and Doctor of Philosophy, the last two being awarded for research in Arts or Sciences.

The University of Cambridge, King's College

The University of Sussex

Degrees are usually awarded by the institution itself. Students of law, architecture and some other professions can take qualifications awarded by their own professional bodies instead of degrees.

In the 1980s the main sources of income for students in higher education were parental contributions and the maintenance grant (money paid by the local authority to cover living expenses, books and travel). By the 1990s this had changed and student loans gradually replaced the old system of grants. By 1999 loans formed 24 per cent of total income for students.

Universities accept students mainly on the basis of their 'A' level results, although they may interview them as well. The Open University was started in 1971 to cater for adults who did not have these formal qualifications. The emphasis has changed in all forms of higher education to include greater numbers of students and encourage people from different backgrounds to apply. In 1970 there were 620,000 students in higher education of whom 33 per cent were women. By 1999 these figures had increased to 2.1 million students of whom 53 per cent were women. Life-long learning skills have also become more important.

Comprehension

Use the information on these two pages to answer the questions.

1 What choices do pupils have at the age of sixteen?
2 If you wanted practical basic training, where would you expect to study in Britain?
3 Which examinations do you need to go to a British university?
4 How do the numbers who go on to higher education in Britain compare with other countries?
5 What have been the major changes in higher education in Britain over the last 25 years?

Discussion

Work in pairs.

1 What are the main differences between university courses in Britain and in your own country?
2 How are college and university courses paid for in your own country?

▪ Going through the system ▪

Introduction

1 Guess what kind of secondary school the speaker went to. The diagram on page 63 may help you.
2 Guess whether the speaker has a university education.

Listening

Listen to the tape and see if you were right. Now answer the following questions.

1 Did the speaker attend a comprehensive school?
2 Was it co–educational?
3 Was it a church school?
4 How did the school help children who left at sixteen?

5 Where did the speaker send his own children to school? How was their school different from his own?
6 Did the speaker's wife have a similar education to his?

Discussion

1 In what sense was the speaker's school 'successful' and in what sense was it 'unsuccessful'?
2 What does the speaker mean when he describes his school as 'a socially divisive institution'?
3 What features do you think a 'successful' school should have?

■ Summary ■

Vocabulary

1 Explain the following expressions.
   pre-school education   post-school
   half-term   National Curriculum
   independent school   Eleven Plus
   compulsory education
   life-long learning   Open University

2 Describe the differences between the
   following pairs.

school	college
primary	secondary
state school	public school
day school	boarding school
pupil	student
undergraduate	postgraduate

Discussion

1 Do you think education should be free? Are
   there advantages in a fee-paying system?
2 Do you think children should be tested at
   the ages of seven and eleven?
3 What are your views of boarding schools?
   Would you like to have attended one
   yourself?
4 How usual is it to go to university in your
   country? Is it difficult to get in? Is a
   university education necessary for
   professional jobs? What other ways are
   there to get professional qualifications?

Writing

1 Using the chart on page 63, draw a diagram
   of the education system in your own
   country.
2 Write a description of your own education.

Boys at school

9

Business and the Economy

▣ Patterns of change ▣

A nation's industries can be divided into three sectors of activity. The primary sector is concerned with raw materials such as cereals and minerals. Processing these materials is the field of the manufacturing sector. The service sector provides services of various kinds such as transport or distribution, but does not manufacture goods. The construction industry can be thought of either as part of the manufacturing sector, or as a separate fourth sector.

Earlier in its history, Britain had a very large manufacturing sector. Food, fuel and raw materials such as cotton were imported in large quantities and paid for with finished goods manufactured in Britain: it was known as 'the workshop of the world'. Today, the manufacturing sector and the small primary sector are employing even fewer people. For example, during the first half of the 1980s the mining and energy industries lost 20 per cent

of their jobs. This was mainly through increases in productivity, so that fewer workers were producing the same output more efficiently. Productivity rose by 14 per cent in the same period in British industry as a whole, although it had previously been low by comparison with other advanced industrial nations. Meanwhile service industries like banking and catering were expanding their workforce.

Britain has a mixed economy, based partly on state ownership but mainly on private enterprise. In the mid-eighties the private

Stock traders in the City of London

Shipbuilding in Sunderland

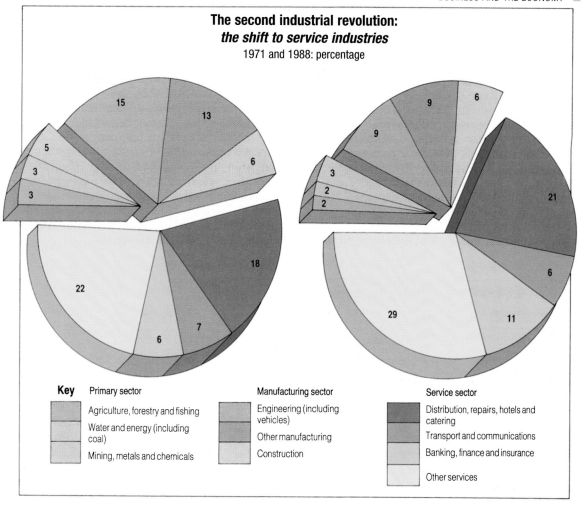

The second industrial revolution:
the shift to service industries
1971 and 1988: percentage

Key

Primary sector
- Agriculture, forestry and fishing
- Water and energy (including coal)
- Mining, metals and chemicals

Manufacturing sector
- Engineering (including vehicles)
- Other manufacturing
- Construction

Service sector
- Distribution, repairs, hotels and catering
- Transport and communications
- Banking, finance and insurance
- Other services

sector accounted for 72 per cent of total employment and 74 per cent of the goods and services produced in Britain. Government policy throughout the 1980s was to sell state-owned industries such as British Telecom and British Airways to private investors, thereby further increasing the size of the private sector.

Comprehension

Use the information on these two pages to answer the questions.

1 What are the three main sectors of industry in any economy?
2 Which sectors of British industry are increasing in size, and which are decreasing?
3 What proportion of the British workforce are involved in manufacturing?
4 Define the following words. Use a dictionary if necessary.
   privatise   state-owned   distribution   catering

Discussion

Work in pairs.

1 What contribution does each sector of the economy make to the production of: a sweater, a hamburger, this book, a telephone call?
2 If British industries continued to change at the same rate, what would you expect them to look like now?

■ Privatisation ■

Britain's energy and transport industries were originally run by companies in the private sector. But in the late 1930s and 1940s these essential services were nationalised under huge state-owned corporations. In later years, the state took over other companies that were in economic difficulties in order to protect jobs: some car manufacturers (including Rolls-Royce) and shipbuilders became state-owned in this way.

From 1979 it was Conservative government policy to return nationalised industries to the private sector. There was considerable political debate about this policy. The Labour Party, which had been responsible for nationalising many industries in the 1940s, felt they should be kept in state ownership. The Conservatives argued that the state ownership had brought no real benefits. They therefore privatised whole industries, such as gas and telecommunications. They also encouraged local authorities, hospitals and schools to use private firms from outside for services such as cleaning and rubbish collection.

INDUSTRIES PRIVATISED BETWEEN 1979 AND 1989
(Each £ represents £1,000,000,000)

Industry	Value	Major privatisations (with dates)
Oil	£££££££££	BP (1987)
		Britoil (1985)
Energy	£££££££££	British Gas (1986)
Communications	£££££	Cable & Wireless (1983)
		British Telecom (1984)
Transport	£££	British Airways (1987)
		British Airports Authority (1987)
Cars	££	Jaguar (1984)
		Rolls-Royce (1987)
Planes	£	British Aerospace (1985)
Others	£	Amersham International (1982)
		Water

OTHER INDUSTRIES PROPOSED FOR PRIVATISATION

Energy	Electricity
Communications	Post Office (counter services, not postal deliveries)
Transport	British Rail
Cars	Austin Rover
Others	Nature reserves
	Helicopter rescue service

(far right) *A poster encouraging people to buy shares in the newly privatised Scottish electricity companies*

FIXED INTEREST

PRICE INDICES	Wed Jul 17	Day's change %	Tue Jul 16	Accrued Interest	xd adj 1991 to date	
British Government						5
Up to 5 years (29)	120.92	+0.01	120.91	1.68	6.71	6
5-15 years (27)	131.72	+0.08	131.61	2.54	7.10	7
Over 15 years (9)	139.17	+0.16	138.95	2.60	6.44	8
Irredeemables (6)	152.45	+0.13	152.23	1.89	7.34	9
All stocks (71)	130.53	+0.06	130.45	2.25	7.02	10 Irre
Index-Linked						Inde 11 Infla
Up to 5 years (1)	159.55	+0.06	159.45	0.59	2.72	12 Inflal
Over 5 years (10)	144.79	+0.18	144.84	0.40	2.76	13 Inflatio
All stocks (11)	145.78	+0.17	145.82	0.41	2.76	14 Inflatio
						15 Debs &
Debs & Loans (56)	109.50	+0.03	109.46	2.57	5.33	16 Loans
						17

FT-ACTUARIES SHAR[E]

© The Financial Times Ltd 1991. Compiled in conjunction with the Institute of Actuaries

EQUITY GROUPS & SUB-SECTIONS figures in parentheses show number of stocks per section	Index No.	Day's Change %	Est. Earnings Yield% (Max.)	Gross Div Yield% (Act a (25%
1 CAPITAL GOODS (184)	815.81		10.63	5.9
2 Building Materials (24)	1036.66		9.41	6.0
3 Contracting, Construction (31)	1145.63		9.61	6.0
4 Electricals (10)	2370.30	+1.5	10.83	5.6
5 Electronics (25)	1705.89	-0.3	8.82	5.5
6 Engineering-Aerospace (8)	407.82	+0.1	16.78	6.1
7 Engineering-General (46)	442.03	+0.6	12.47	5.6
8 Metals and Metal Forming (8)	438.80	+1.8	16.08	8.0
9 Motors (12)	318.49	+1.2	12.41	7.5
0 Other Industrial Materials (20)	1561.03	-0.9	8.93	5.1
1 CONSUMER GROUP (187)	1502.18	+0.1	7.81	3.6
2 Brewers and Distillers (22)	1838.48	+0.3	8.37	3.6
5 Food Manufacturing (19)	1177.52	-0.7	9.74	4.2
6 Food Retailing (17)	2761.29	+1.2	7.80	3.0
7 Health and Household (22)	3661.52	-0.3	5.20	2.3
9 Hotels and Leisure (23)	1238.18	+0.1	10.27	5.6
0 Media (26)	1409.26	+0.1	9.08	4.9
1 Packaging, Paper & Printing (17)	721.07	+0.6	7.80	4.5
4 Stores (32)	936.23		8.28	3.8
5 Textiles (9)	551.11	+0.2	9.10	5.6
0 OTHER GROUPS (109)	1234.67	-0.1	10.14	5.2
1 Business Services (12)	1280.82	-0.2	8.95	5.4
2 Chemicals (21)	1407.37		8.01	5.1
3 Conglomerates (10)	1436.22	+0.1	10.61	5.2
4 Transport (13)	2167.15	+0.2	8.73	4.9
5 Electricity (16)	1198.96	-0.3	14.40	5.6
6 Telephone Networks(4)	1466.55		10.11	4.1
7 Water(10)	2332.42	+1.0	17.57	6.6
8 Miscellaneous (23)	2010.02	-0.5	6.02	4.8
9 INDUSTRIAL GROUP (480)	1249.14		9.10	4.5
1 Oil & Gas (20)	2491.88	+0.9	10.89	5.5
9 500 SHARE INDEX (500)	1353.75	+0.1	9.33	4.6
1 FINANCIAL GROUP (94)	799.20	+0.5		5.9
2 Banks (9)	926.64	+1.1	6.47	6.5

■ Share ownership ■

The sale of state-owned industries meant that share ownership increased. State corporations were turned into companies whose shares could be bought and sold on the stock market. For example British Telecom and British Gas shares were sold to the general public with huge advertising campaigns. On the other hand the National Freight Corporation was initially bought from the state by its own employees to preserve their jobs: shares were not available to the general public until five years later.

In 1979 less than a third of shares in the London stock market were owned by private individuals. The rest were owned by large financial institutions such as insurance companies, and the proportion of individuals owning shares had fallen far behind the rate in other western industrial countries. Privatisation altered the picture dramatically. However, it is impossible to say whether share ownership has made individuals generally richer as that depends on the state of the stock market at any given time.

Comprehension

Use the information on these two pages to answer the questions.

1 What is the difference between privatisation and nationalisation?
2 Which major industries were privatised after 1980?
3 What proportion of shares were owned by individuals in 1979?
4 How did personal share ownership change after 1980?

Discussion

Work in pairs.

1 Compare the dates on the table and the diagram and decide which privatisations had an important effect on share ownership.
2 What advantages and disadvantages can you see in privatisation? Are there any examples of privatised or nationalised industries in your own country?

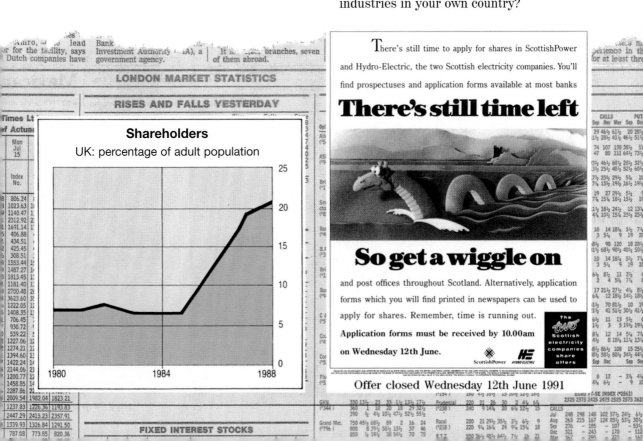

■ The City of London ■

London has been an important centre for finance for many years. The financial district, known simply as 'the City', occupies one square mile of central London. It is the site of the original walled city, and still has its own Lord Mayor and local government. Until very recently it was the home of the 'City gent' with black bowler hat and tightly rolled umbrella; the bowler is rarely seen today. In contrast to the entertainment district in the West End of London, the City is almost deserted at night. Although hundreds of thousands of people work in its offices by day, only about eight thousand actually live within the square mile.

Although the City is central to international finance, to many observers it seems increasingly independent of the British domestic economy. When London was an imperial capital, the City was its financial heart, but in the age of telecommunications, the City could be situated anywhere.

(below) *The Bank of England* (centre) *The Stock Exchange* (right) *Lloyd's of London*

The Bank of England

This is Britain's central reserve bank. It controls other British banks, issues banknotes (although the Scottish banks still issue their own notes), and acts as the government's banker. The City has the greatest concentration of banks in the world and is responsible for about a quarter of international bank lending.

The Stock Exchange

London has had a Stock Exchange for dealing in stocks and shares for over 200 years. Since 1973 it has been the single International Stock Exchange for the United Kingdom and the Republic of Ireland. In March 1986 membership of the London Stock Exchange was opened to overseas companies, and commissions became negotiable. In October 1986 it became possible for stockbrokers to deal in shares through telephones and computers instead of face-to-face on the floor of the Exchange. These dramatic changes in City practices became known as 'Big Bang':

BUSINESS AND THE ECONOMY ■ 75

they linked London much more closely with the other major international financial centres in Tokyo and New York.

A number of international exchanges are also based in the City. These provide an international market where materials and services can be bought and sold. For example, the London Metal Exchange deals in industrial metals and the Baltic Exchange arranges the sale of half of the world's ships and most of the world's sea cargo.

Lloyd's of London

The City is also a major centre for insurance services. Lloyd's of London insures everything from houses to ships through its underwriters, insurance specialists who accept risks on behalf of groups of members who are responsible for meeting any insurance claims. Lloyd's currently receives £8,000 million in payments each year, 75 per cent from outside Britain. Lloyd's also publishes detailed information on ships and their movements.

Comprehension

Use the information on these two pages to answer the questions.

1 What exactly is 'the City'?
2 Name four of the City's major financial institutions.
3 Where do 'underwriters' work? What do they do?
4 When was 'Big Bang'? What changes were introduced?

Discussion

Work in pairs.

1 Which institutions mentioned above would be likely to have the following information:
   a the number of £10 notes in circulation in Britain?
   b the international price of copper?
   c the cost of transporting goods by sea?
   d the cost of insuring a ship?
2 Which of the City's activities are connected with the international world of finance, and which are related to Britain's own economy?

■ A City gent ■

Introduction

1 Where is Lloyd's?
2 What is its function?

Listening

1 What does Lloyd's insure?
2 Match the definitions with the insurance expressions.
   a people with the money   underwriters
   b specialists who write risks cargoes
   c things which are insured   'names'
   d collections of 'names'   risks
   e what ships, etc. carry   syndicates

3 Put these stages of Lloyd's development in the correct order:
   a exchanging news about ships
   b moving to the Royal Exchange
   c computerisation and decentralisation
   d insuring each other against losses
   e meeting at Edward Lloyd's coffee house

Discussion

Work in pairs.

1 What differences have computers made to Lloyd's?
2 What would Edward Lloyd recognise in the Lloyd's of today?

■ Summary ■

Vocabulary

1 Match each expression in the first column with its opposite in the second. Give an example of each.

a domestic   manufacturing
b raw materials   state–owned
c privatisation   finished goods
d primary sector   nationalisation
e private   international

2 Give an example of a job connected with each of the following:

     a nationalised industry   Lloyd's
     the Stock Exchange   the private sector
     British Airways   British Telecom   BP
     the retail trade   the catering industry

Building new offices in London's Docklands

Discussion

1 Britain has been described as 'the first post-industrial society'. What trends described in this unit would support that view?
2 Which changes described in this unit are also found in other countries?
3 Which industries do you think should be controlled by the state and which by private shareholders? Give reasons for your choices.

Writing

Summarise the changes in the British economy. Include the changes mentioned in each section of this unit. Compare the situation in Britain with your own country.

10

Employment

■ Industry and the workforce ■

Young people going to work in the City of London

Young people out of work in the North of England

By the year 2000 Britain's working population – the workforce – was 27 million (nearly 50 per cent of the total population). Those in employment include full-time, part-time and self-employed people.

People are employed in the three sectors mentioned in unit 9: primary, manufacturing and service. Employment is also often divided into sections according to types of work and social class. These categories include professional, manual and non-manual. A doctor, for example, would be classed as a professional in the service sector, while a steelworker would be a manual worker (skilled or unskilled) in the manufacturing sector. The old distinction between white-collar (non-manual) and blue-collar (manual) workers has become less clear as Britain's heavy industry has declined and new technology has become more important. In general, one trend is very clear: fewer people now make cars or work in coal mines; more

work for banks and hotels.

In 1951 96 per cent of the people in work in Britain had full-time jobs and the majority of these (70 per cent) were held by men. By 2000 21 per cent of jobs were part-time and 44 per cent of workers were women. The basic employment trend of the 1980s continued, with a general rise in the number of part-time jobs for women, particularly in service industries. The number of people who were self-employed also rose due partly to new technologies and to changing work patterns. The high unemployment of the 1980s fell during the 1990s.

As well as regional and occupational variations there are big differences in pay between men and women. The average full-time wage for women is still only 80 per cent of the male average, even when the same job is involved. Certain highly-paid occupations such as surgery are still almost exclusively confined to men.

SOCIAL CLASSES
The Institute of Practitioners In Advertising (IPA) define six social classes, based on the occupation of the head of household

Class	Occupation
A	Higher managerial, administrative, or professional
B	Intermediate managerial, administrative, or professional
C1	Supervisory or clerical, junior managerial, administrative, or professional
C2	Skilled manual workers
D	Semi and unskilled manual workers
E	State pensioners, casual or lowest grade workers, or long-term unemployed

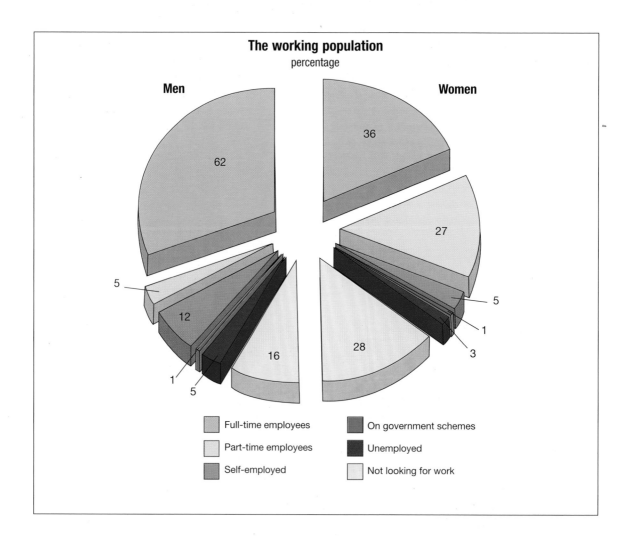

The working population
percentage

Men

62

5

12

1

5

16

Women

36

27

5

1

3

28

- Full-time employees
- Part-time employees
- Self-employed
- On government schemes
- Unemployed
- Not looking for work

Comprehension

Use the information on pages 78 to 80 to answer the questions.

1 How many people in Britain had jobs at the end of the 1990s? Which categories of work are mentioned?
2 In which industrial areas did the number of workers (a) decline and (b) increase?
3 What examples of jobs are given in the text and how are they classified?
4 Are there any differences between the average earnings of men and women in Britain?

Discussion

Work in pairs.

1 Explain the following: a white-collar worker, a surgeon, the workforce, self-employed.
2 Which sector of industry would the following people be involved in: a nurse, a shipbuilder, a waitress, a building-site foreman, a secretary, a farmer, a teacher, a factory worker, a bank manager?
3 Make comparisons between the figures for male and female workers in the diagram.

■ Patterns of employment ■

During the 1980s high unemployment was a political and social problem which refused to go away. In 1986 the overall figure was nearly 10 per cent of the workforce but by the end of the 1990s unemployment had fallen to 4.5 per cent. While old industries continued to decline new technology offered opportunities for employment in, for example, work with computers and new services such as call centres and financial advice. The workforce became more flexible and the old idea of a 'job for life' began to disappear. Re-training programmes and schemes for people to learn 'life-long skills' became more important. The Labour government elected in 1997 placed great emphasis on the importance of work, partly as a way of reducing the dependence on welfare state benefits.

NEW JOBS

Information Technology
In 2000 there were 855,000 people working in Information Technology, an increase of 45% in five years.

Call centres
By 2001 there were 7,000 call centres in the UK employing more than 400,000 staff. This figure is estimated to rise to 665,000 by 2008.

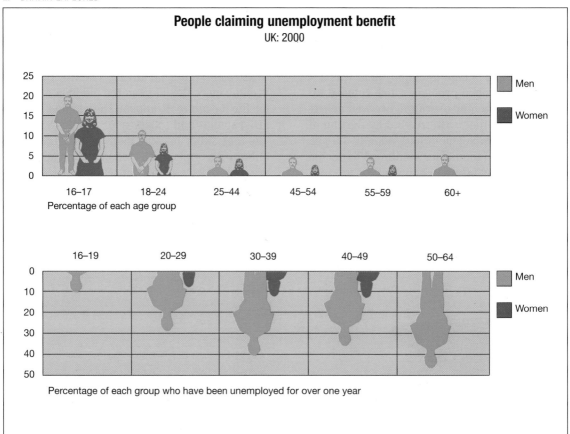

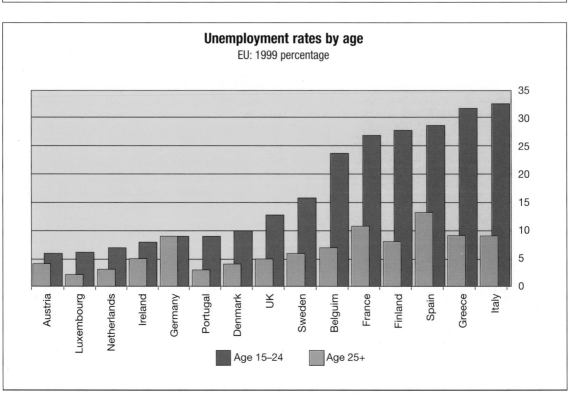

Comprehension

Use the information on pages 81 and 82 to answer the questions.

1 How did unemployment change between 1979 and 2000 according to government figures?
2 What happened to old industries?
3 Explain: a 'job for life' and a 'call centre'.
4 Where were the highest and lowest EU rates of unemployment?
5 Which age groups were most likely to be unemployed in Britain in 2000?

Discussion

Work in pairs.

1 Compare the rate of unemployment in Britain with other countries.
2 Which areas of your country have suffered most from unemployment? What sort of industries have had the most problems? What new industries have appeared?

■ At work ■

For many people with jobs, there was an improvement in pay and working conditions. The amount of holidays increased (for example over three-quarters of all manual employees had between four and five weeks' paid holiday per year) and the average working week, excluding overtime, fell to under 40 hours. A minimum hourly wage was introduced in April 1999 and European legislation began to affect the working conditions including the age of retirement (traditionally 65 for men and 60 for women) and the number of hours people are allowed to work in a week.

The Durham Miners' Gala

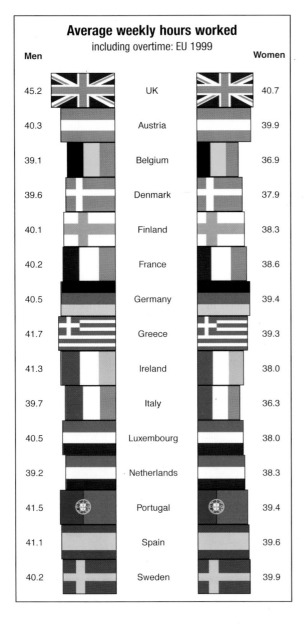

Average weekly hours worked
including overtime: EU 1999

Men		Women
45.2	UK	40.7
40.3	Austria	39.9
39.1	Belgium	36.9
39.6	Denmark	37.9
40.1	Finland	38.3
40.2	France	38.6
40.5	Germany	39.4
41.7	Greece	39.3
41.3	Ireland	38.0
39.7	Italy	36.3
40.5	Luxembourg	38.0
39.2	Netherlands	38.3
41.5	Portugal	39.4
41.1	Spain	39.6
40.2	Sweden	39.9

For many, working conditions improved and carrying on from the 'enterprise economy' of the 1980s some people did very well, particularly those involved in new technologies. Others, especially women and part-time workers in the service industries, were not so lucky. Industrial relations continued to be an area of dispute but there was a large decrease in the number of strikes. This was partly due to new laws passed during the 1980s and 1990s. Some industrial action still occurred where job cuts were announced, as a result of international or global trends, or actions by large companies to reduce costs. 'Down-sizing', 'relocation' and 'rationalisation' were all terms commonly used during the 1990s.

What different people earn
1986 figures: wages have risen by about 50% since then

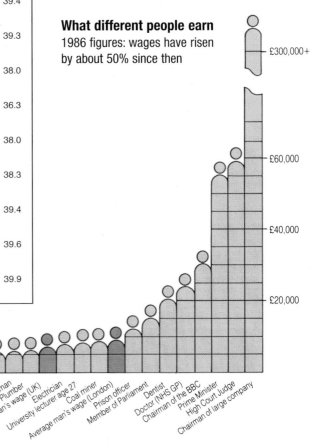

£300,000+

£60,000

£40,000

£20,000

1st year student nurse
Farm labourer
Shop assistant
Average woman's wage (UK)
Butcher
Newly qualified teacher
Average woman's wage (London)
Car salesman
Car mechanic
Postman
Plumber
Average man's wage (UK)
Electrician
University lecturer age 27
Coal miner
Average man's wage (London)
Prison officer
Member of Parliament
Dentist
Doctor (NHS GP)
Chairman of the BBC
Prime Minister
High Court Judge
Chairman of large company

Working days lost due to strikes

Strikes fell everywhere in the 1980s. In 1986 Britain had fewer strikes than in any year since 1939.

Annual average per 1,000 workers 1972-81

Italy · Canada · Australia · UK · USA · Denmark · France · Sweden · Norway · Netherlands · W Germany

Comprehension

Use the information on pages 83 to 85 to answer the questions.

1 For most workers in Britain what has happened to:
  a the working week?
  b paid holidays?
  c the standard of living?
2 Who benefited least from the 'enterprise economy'?
3 What sort of jobs are the best paid and the worst paid in Britain?
4 What do 'down-sizing' and 'rationalisation' mean? Why are international and global trends important?

Discussion

Work in pairs.

1 What sort of jobs pay the most and the least in your country?
2 Is Britain's reputation as a country with lots of strikes still justified? What happens in your country when there is an industrial dispute? Are there any laws against strikes?

■ Self-employment ■

Introduction

1 What do you understand by 'self-employment'?
2 What advantages might there be in self-employment?
3 What disadvantages might there be?

Listening

1 What does the speaker sell? In which town?
2 Why isn't his shop in a main street?
3 Why did he and his wife start the shop?
4 Have they been successful?
5 What are the problems with setting up a small business?

6 What did the speaker need:
   a from educational publishers?
   b from a bank manager?
7 Who tells the self-employed person what to do?
8 What do you think 'tipping your cap to someone' means?

Discussion

Work in pairs.

1 What advantages and disadvantages of self-employment are mentioned?
2 Are they the same as the ones you listed in the *Introduction*?

■ Summary ■

Vocabulary

1 Make a list of twelve jobs. Use the information in this unit to help you. Then put them in order:
   a according to how well paid they are in Britain.
   b according to how important you think they are to society.
2 Where do your twelve jobs fit into these categories:
   a professional/non-manual/manual?
   b primary/manufacturing/service?
   e.g. a nurse is a non-manual worker in a service industry.

Discussion

1 What major changes took place in employment in the UK in the 1980s and 1990s?
2 How important do you think trade unions are? What positive or negative effects do you think they have on work and employment?
3 What, in your opinion, are the best ways to prepare young people to help them get a job?
4 If you became unemployed how would you spend your time?

Writing

Write a paragraph describing the job you would most like to do. Explain your reasons.

A Job Centre

11

The Family

A Victorian family

A modern family

Family structure

The British live longer, marry later, have fewer children and are more likely to get divorced than ever before. Young people leave home earlier, though not necessarily to get married. More women now go out to work and more people, especially the old, live alone. The nuclear family (parents and perhaps two children) has largely replaced the extended family where several generations lived together, but has also been partly replaced by patterns of remarriage where children with different parents may live together as a family for some or all of the time.

Although patterns are changing, most people in Britain still get married and have children and stay together until the end of their lives. People are marrying later: the average woman gets married at twenty-seven to a man who is just over two years older (although it is estimated that 40 per cent of

couples live together before getting married). Mrs Average now has her first child in her late twenties, but she will have only one or two children: only one mother in four has more. Eight out of ten married women will have children at some point in their lives. And despite the changes in working habits it is usually the woman who has overall responsibility for domestic life: the traditional division of family responsibilities still persists.

Britain has one of the highest divorce rates in Western Europe: approximately one in three marriages end in divorce, half of them in the first ten years of marriage. As a result more people are getting remarried and there are now over 1.6 million single parents. There has also been a sharp rise in the rate of illegitimacy; by 1999 nearly 40 per cent of babies were born outside marriage.

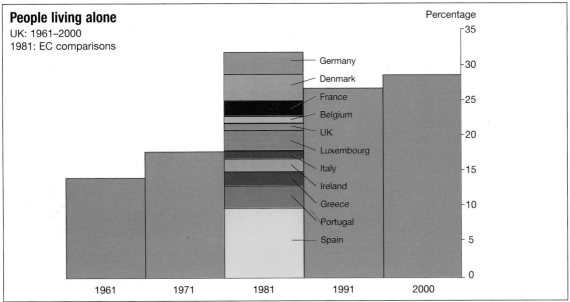

People living alone
UK: 1961–2000
1981: EC comparisons

Percentage

Germany
Denmark
France
Belgium
UK
Luxembourg
Italy
Ireland
Greece
Portugal
Spain

1961 1971 1981 1991 2000

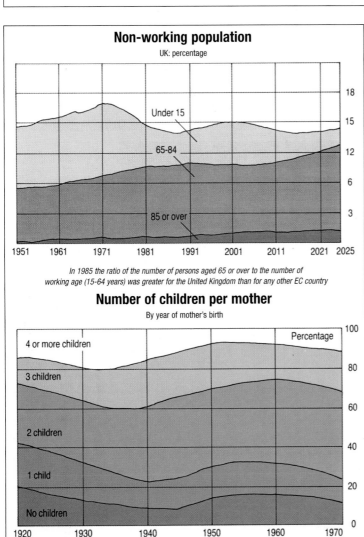

Non-working population
UK: percentage

Under 15

65-84

85 or over

1951 1961 1971 1981 1991 2001 2011 2021 2025

In 1985 the ratio of the number of persons aged 65 or over to the number of working age (15-64 years) was greater for the United Kingdom than for any other EC country

Number of children per mother
By year of mother's birth

Percentage

4 or more children

3 children

2 children

1 child

No children

1920 1930 1940 1950 1960 1970

Comprehension

Use the information on these two pages to answer the questions.

1 Find four trends in family structure mentioned in the text.
2 At what age do people in Britain get married on average?
3 What is the difference between a nuclear and an extended family?
4 Explain the following:
   a illegitimacy
   b remarriage
   c single parent

Discussion

Work in pairs.

1 What sort of people are most likely to live alone in Britain? What are the reasons for this?
2 How does the number of children per family in Britain compare with your country? How big is your own family?

Parents

A 'white wedding' in church

A registry office wedding

Although the number of people who have a 'white wedding' is decreasing, many people still prefer to get married in church.

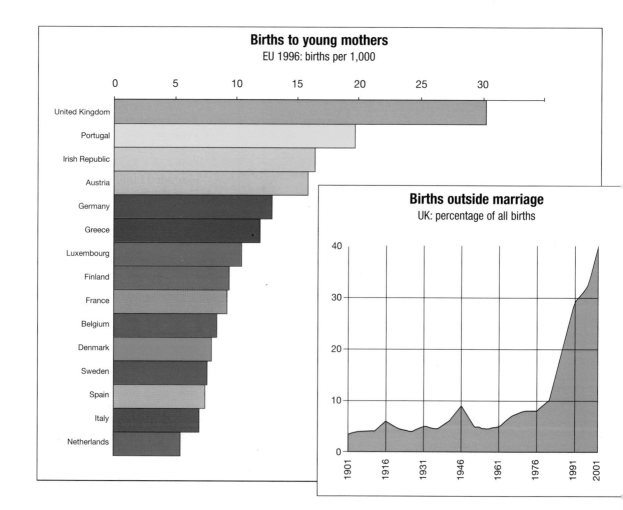

Births to young mothers
EU 1996: births per 1,000

United Kingdom
Portugal
Irish Republic
Austria
Germany
Greece
Luxembourg
Finland
France
Belgium
Denmark
Sweden
Spain
Italy
Netherlands

Births outside marriage
UK: percentage of all births

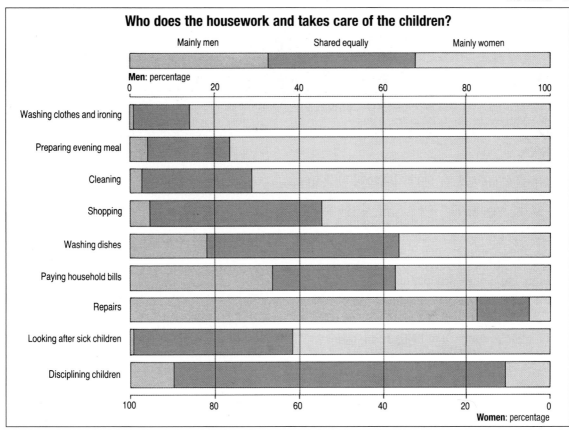

Who does the housework and takes care of the children?

Mainly men · Shared equally · Mainly women

Men: percentage
0 · 20 · 40 · 60 · 80 · 100

- Washing clothes and ironing
- Preparing evening meal
- Cleaning
- Shopping
- Washing dishes
- Paying household bills
- Repairs
- Looking after sick children
- Disciplining children

100 · 80 · 60 · 40 · 20 · 0
Women: percentage

Working mothers

In 1931 less than 10 per cent of married women were in employment: over the last thirty years the proportion of married women working has increased from 21 per cent to over 50 per cent. More than a quarter of women with children under the age of five and about two-thirds of women with school-age children go out to work.

Women generally are spending a larger proportion of their lives in paid employment. It is now normal for a woman to be in full-time work until the birth of the first child, and an increasingly high proportion of women return to work after having a child, although this may be to a part-time job. Women are also returning to work more quickly after having a child. Britain has a high percentage of working mothers compared to some other countries (for example Italy, Ireland and Japan) but provisions for maternity leave and child care are amongst the lowest in Europe.

Comprehension

Use the information on these two pages to answer the questions.

1 Where can you get married in Britain?
2 What do the figures on marriage and divorce tell you about the modern family in Britain?
3 What percentage of children are born outside marriage?
4 What percentage of mothers go out to work in Britain?

Discussion

Work in pairs.

1 Why do you think many British couples still get married in church?
2 What conclusions can you make about who does the housework in a British family? How does this compare with what happens in your family?

■ Young people ■

Despite media reports, not all young people in Britain are punks or football hooligans. There is a wide cross-section of youth from Young Conservatives to Rastafarians, from skinheads to pupils at expensive private schools.

Nineteenth-century, Victorian attitudes about how children should be brought up have largely disappeared and for many children family life has become more relaxed and less strict. Many young people in Britain have a considerable amount of freedom and the things they are interested in reflect this: music, computers, television, shopping, sex, fashion and money predominate. Being independent and free to choose are priorities. Attitudes towards religion and marriage have changed and for many children there is a much higher standard of living than even twenty years ago. Ever since the media discovered the world of the teenager, films, videos, TV programmes and magazines have all been marketed towards the young.

There are a number of social problems associated with being young: some schools have problems with discipline and motivation; crime and drug-taking in some areas have reached serious levels. Employment prospects for young people who leave school early or without qualifications are not good. The new consumer society means that many children do not take much exercise; many including quite young children are overweight.

For many young people leaving home is a route to independence, although for some this may be financially impossible. Most young couples hope to be able to have their own house or flat: in modern Britain financial pressures are much more likely to restrict this than family pressure.

AGES YOU CAN LEGALLY DO THINGS	
Leave school	16
Ride a small motorbike	16
Buy cigarettes	16
Get married (with parents' consent)	16
Drive a car	17
Buy alcohol	18
Vote	18
Get married (without parents' consent)	18

Comprehension

Use the information on these two pages to answer the questions.

1 What examples can you find in the text of different types of British young people? What are young people in Britain interested in?

2 At what age in Britain can you do the following:
  a drive a car?
  b get married?
  c buy alcohol?
  d leave school?

3 What are the main issues that concern the eight young people on page 93?

I'm at boarding school where there are lots of rules and regulations. During the holidays I'm allowed to stay out until 11.30 at night.

The main thing I argue about with my parents is money. Most of my friends get more pocket money than me.

I hated school. They were always trying to make us do things. It was boring.

Listening to music is the thing I enjoy most. My parents didn't like the kind of clothes I wear at first but now they've got used to it.

The worst thing about not having a job is having no money. I'd like to leave home and be more independent but it's just not possible.

My parents wanted me to stay at school and get more qualifications but at least I've got a job.

My parents are much stricter than a lot of my friends' parents. They don't like me going to discos.

Discussion

Work in pairs.

1 Do you think young people have more freedom in Britain than in your country? When do people in your country leave home, for example? Is it easy for them to find somewhere to live?
2 What do/did you and your parents argue about? How many of the issues mentioned on these two pages are/were important?

I moved away from home when I came to university. It's difficult financially but apart from that it's great.

■ A working mother ■

Introduction

The speaker is a teacher and mother of three young children.

1 Is it usual for mothers to go out to work in Britain? (See page 91.)
2 What are the advantages of teaching as a job for a working mother?

Listening

1 Put these parts of the speaker's life in the correct order:
   a full-time housewife
   b training to be a teacher
   c teaching in nursery schools
   d full-time teacher of handicapped children
   e part-time 'supply' teaching

2 What sort of work does she do with physically handicapped children?
3 When do her children help? Why?
4 What is the 'horrible dilemma' that working mothers have to face?
5 What are the other two main difficulties she mentions?
6 How does she feel that her children benefit from her working?

Discussion

Work in pairs.

1 What advantages has the speaker had, which have allowed her to work and raise a family?
2 Do you think women with children should be in full-time employment?

■ Summary ■

Vocabulary

1 Find a word or phrase which is opposite in meaning to these expressions used in the unit:

   full-time   nuclear family   go out to work
   married   increasing   strict

2 Make a list of as many English words for relatives as you can (e.g. *father, mother,* etc). Then draw a family tree for your own family.

Discussion

1 One in three marriages in Britain ends in divorce. What effects might this have on society and children? How easy do you think it should be to get a divorce?

2 What are the advantages and disadvantages of an extended family system? Is there the same problem with old people living alone in your country?

3 In your view what are the most important aspects which keep families together?

Writing

Prepare six questions related to aspects of family life. Then ask as many people in your class as possible to give you their answers. Report your findings.

12

The Cost of Living

■ Trends ■

Family expenditure patterns in Britain changed during the 1980s and 1990s, with households spending a smaller proportion of their income on food and more on housing and transport than they had done twenty years earlier. Rises in house prices and the increase in the number of people owning their own home contributed to this trend. More people drove cars, shopped in big supermarkets and had bank accounts. As the standard of living rose for many people, spending on leisure activities such as holidays went up, and items which had previously been considered luxuries were seen as necessities.

The number of people owning consumer goods such as washing machines and video recorders increased as did the number of households with telephones, televisions, computers and central heating. On the other hand the worst-off were the unemployed, single parents and people living on the state pension. In 1999 the basic pension was only one quarter of the average national wage and it was estimated that many pensioners were having to spend two-thirds of their income on housing, fuel and food.

Inflation fell to below 3 per cent but the strong pound caused problems for business and there were disagreements about Britain joining the European Monetary System. The use of consumer credit in the form of credit-cards and bank loans became more common. The gap between the rich and the poor continued to become wider during the 1990s although for many there was a better overall standard of living.

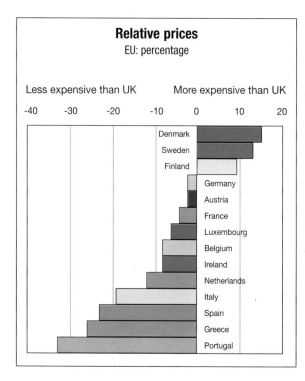

Relative prices
EU: percentage

Less expensive than UK   More expensive than UK

-40   -30   -20   -10   0   10   20

Denmark
Sweden
Finland
Germany
Austria
France
Luxembourg
Belgium
Ireland
Netherlands
Italy
Spain
Greece
Portugal

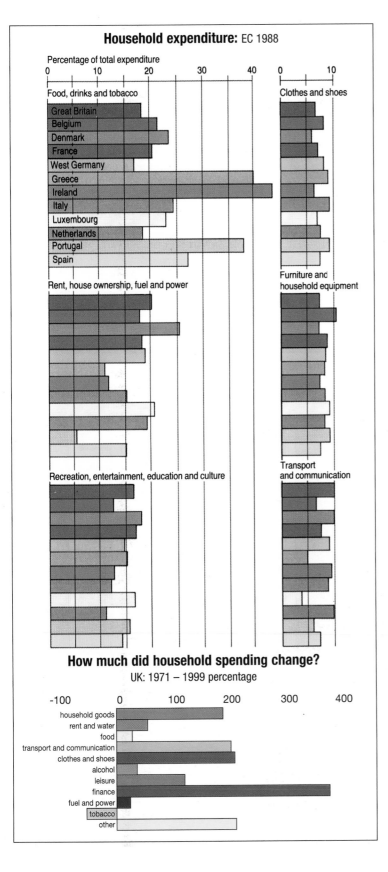

Household expenditure: EC 1988

Percentage of total expenditure

Food, drinks and tobacco
- Great Britain
- Belgium
- Denmark
- France
- West Germany
- Greece
- Ireland
- Italy
- Luxembourg
- Netherlands
- Portugal
- Spain

Clothes and shoes

Rent, house ownership, fuel and power

Furniture and household equipment

Recreation, entertainment, education and culture

Transport and communication

How much did household spending change?

UK: 1971 – 1999 percentage

- household goods
- rent and water
- food
- transport and communication
- clothes and shoes
- alcohol
- leisure
- finance
- fuel and power
- tobacco
- other

Comprehension

Use the information on these two pages to answer the questions.

1 Explain the following:
   a credit
   b consumer goods
   c pensioners
   d pay claims
2 What were people more likely to spend their money on during the 1980s and 1990s?
3 What features of the British economy are mentioned?
4 What examples are given of worrying features in the British economy?

Discussion

Work in pairs.

1 How did consumer price rises in Britain compare with other countries in Europe?
2 According to the diagrams what were the main changes in British spending patterns? How did the new patterns compare with those in other European countries?

■ Rich and poor ■

Income distribution has not changed much since the 1970s but the sources of income have changed considerably. Income from employment has dropped while income from activities such as saving, renting property, and investing in the stock market has risen. The proportion of money spent on private health care and private pensions has gone up. The amount of money spent on pensions and benefits by the welfare state has also risen but this is mainly the result of an ageing population.

A major aim of Conservative economic policy during the 1980s was to reduce direct taxation and the Labour government continued this policy. In practice however, the percentage of income which goes in taxes has actually risen since the 1970s. This is partly because tax thresholds (income levels at which people have to pay a certain rate of tax) have not risen as fast as income, and also because there has been an increase in indirect taxation, for example on the cost of fuel.

INCOME TAX IN THE UK: 2001/02

10% up to £1,880 a year
22% up to £29,400 a year
40% above £29,400 a year

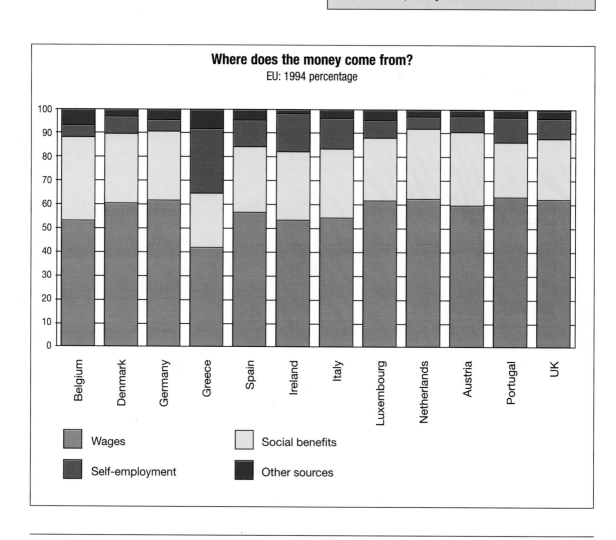

Where does the money come from?
EU: 1994 percentage

Legend:
- Wages
- Self-employment
- Social benefits
- Other sources

Countries (left to right): Belgium, Denmark, Germany, Greece, Spain, Ireland, Italy, Luxembourg, Netherlands, Austria, Portugal, UK

A homeless man in London

Elton John, a wealthy popstar

The rich

The richest people in the world are worth tens of billions of pounds. Official figures show that there are more than 300,000 UK tax payers who earn more than £100,000 a year. The richest people in Britain include pop stars, supermarket owners, comedians, actors, writers, inventors and members of the aristocracy and the Royal Family. Their wealth is calculated on the value of their property, land, shares and other assets. The Queen (£16 billion) is one of the richest people in Britain. Paul McCartney is the world's first pop star billionaire.

The poor

The worst-off people in Britain are the long-term unemployed, single parents, the homeless, some ethnic groups and some pensioners.

Poverty is difficult to measure. Official UK figures suggest you are poor if your household income is below 60 per cent of the average. In 1999 in Britain 18 per cent of people (24 per cent of children – 3.1 million) were living in such households. Where you live can also make a big difference and women are worse off than men. On average and despite thirty years of Equal Opportunities legislation women's pay is still less than men's.

Comprehension

Use the information on these two pages to answer the questions.

1 Has income distribution changed?
2 What is the difference between direct and indirect taxation?
3 What are the main sources of income shown in the diagram?
4 What sort of people in Britain become very rich?

Discussion

Work in pairs.

1 What forms of taxation are there in Britain? How much tax do people pay? Is the system similar in your country?
2 Has the standard of living changed in your country? Give some examples.

■ The consumer society ■

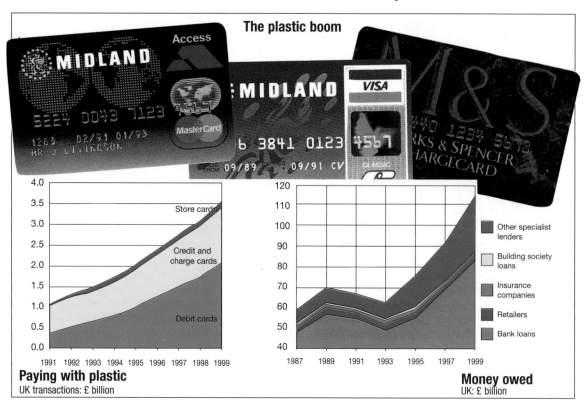

The plastic boom

Paying with plastic
UK transactions: £ billion

Store cards
Credit and charge cards
Debit cards

Money owed
UK: £ billion

Other specialist lenders
Building society loans
Insurance companies
Retailers
Bank loans

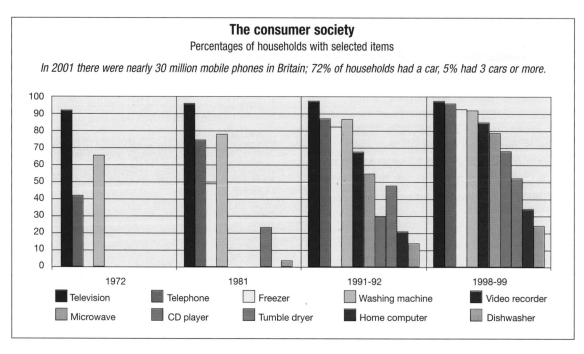

The consumer society
Percentages of households with selected items

In 2001 there were nearly 30 million mobile phones in Britain; 72% of households had a car, 5% had 3 cars or more.

1972   1981   1991-92   1998-99

■ Television   ■ Telephone   □ Freezer   ■ Washing machine   ■ Video recorder
■ Microwave   ■ CD player   ■ Tumble dryer   ■ Home computer   ■ Dishwasher

HOW LONG DO YOU WORK TO PAY FOR THINGS?

Weekly wage	£370.00	25-34-year-old with higher education
Hours worked	45.20	UK male average: see page 84
Wage per minute	£0.14	Wage divided by hours divided by 60
After tax	£0.11	Standard rate 22%: see page 98

sliced white bread: 5 mins

250g butter: 8 mins

1 pint milk (0.57l): 3 mins

12 medium eggs: 15 mins

100g instant coffee: 20 mins

1 pint beer(0.57l): 19 mins

20 cigarettes: 43 mins

1 litre unleaded petrol: 8 mins

Weekly bills

gas: 1 hr 3 mins

electricity: 56 mins

water: 1 hr 1 min

phone: 1 hr 35 mins*

*including internet & cable

Comprehension

Use the information on these two pages to answer the questions.

1 What method of payment became popular in the 1980s and 1990s for the purchase of consumer goods?
2 How did the amount of credit debt rise?
3 Look at the chart on page 100. What percentage of households had the following in 1999: a TV; a telephone; a washing machine; a computer? How have the figures changed since 1972?
4 How long, on average, do the British work to pay for these items: a loaf of bread; a pint of beer; a dozen eggs; a litre of petrol?

Discussion

Work in pairs.

1 Do you think it is a good thing for people to be able to buy goods on credit? What are the advantages and disadvantages?
2 How do the items in the diagrams on these two pages compare with your country? Which are the cheapest? Which are the most expensive?

◼ Living on a pension ◼

Introduction

1 How old do you think men and women must be in Britain to get a state pension?
2 Do you think this pensioner enjoys her retirement?
3 Do you think she has any experience of poverty?

Listening

Listen to the tape and see if you were right. Now answer the following questions.

1 Does the speaker live in a large house?
2 Which of the following sources of income does she mention:
    investments property savings
    part-time work state pension
    company pension
3 Which of the above does she receive income from?
4 What difference does it make that she is a 'war widow'?
5 What did her experience as a social worker teach her?
6 How would you explain 'I'm all right, Jack'?
7 What sort of entertainment does she enjoy?
8 What does she do that she feels is useful?

Discussion

Work in pairs.

1 Why is life more expensive for the poor?
2 Which is better, in your opinion: work or retirement?

■ Summary ■

Vocabulary

1 Look at this list of words and divide them into two categories:
  a words which describe groups of people
  b words connected with finance and money
  credit   pensioners   wealth   poverty
  millionaires   consumers   income
  wages   pension   employees   prices
  government   families   inflation   taxes
  households   investing   expenditure
2 Look back through this unit and make a list of twelve things which people buy. Then put them in order according to:
  a the cost (start with the most expensive)
  b how necessary they are for everyday life.

Discussion

1 Do you agree that life has become easier for people in Britain? What examples can you give?
2 Which groups of people in your country are the least well-off? Is the situation the same as in Britain?
3 How much tax do you think people should pay? What sorts of goods and services do you think should be taxed?

Writing

What differences are there between the possessions that people have now and those they had twenty years ago? Write a description of the consumer goods that you have in your family and how things have changed.

Consumer goods

13 Housing

▨ Patterns of housing ▨

Nearly 70 per cent of people in Britain live in their own homes, about one fifth live in property rented from local councils or registered landlords and ten per cent live in privately-rented accommodation. The figures vary with different ages (the figure for 16–24 year-olds in private rented accommodation was nearly 40 per cent in 2000). The total number of dwellings is nearly 25 million and houses are much more common than flats (the ratio is approximately four to one). Nearly two-thirds of homes in England were built after 1945.

The number of houses being built and the number of people who own their own homes have both increased. In 1951 only 4 million dwellings were owned by the people who lived in them; by 2000 it was more than 16 million and still rising. Under the Conservative government in the 1980s many people who previously rented their homes from the local council were given the opportunity to buy them. It is generally cheaper in the long term to buy a home than to rent one but purchasers need to find a deposit in order to get a

mortgage and for many young people buying a house is impossible because they are too expensive. This is especially true in some parts of England, particularly the south-east, and the selling-off of council property has reduced the amount of cheap housing available. House prices tend to adjust according to how much money people are earning (with occasional 'booms' in property prices). In Britain the cost of buying somewhere to live varies considerably according to the area.

Buying a house is a large financial investment for many people and the majority buy their homes with a mortgage loan from a building society or bank. The loan is repaid in monthly instalments over a period of twenty years or more. Some people rent or buy accommodation through housing associations which provide a financial alternative to the mortgage system. There has also been an increase in the amount of accommodation for single householders, particularly older people, as the number of pensioners has increased. Accommodation known as 'sheltered' housing

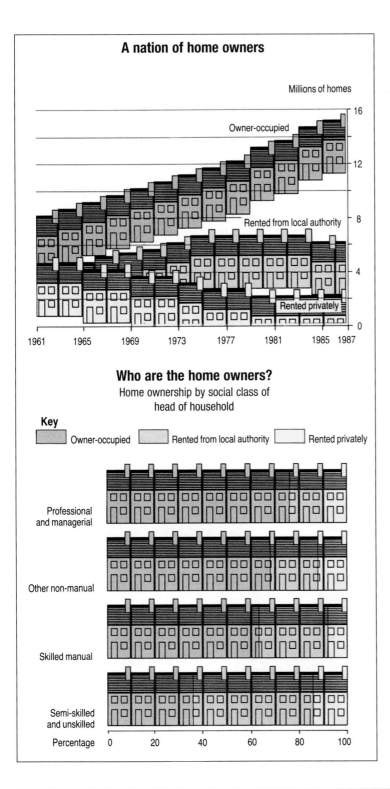

A nation of home owners

Millions of homes

Owner-occupied

Rented from local authority

Rented privately

1961 1965 1969 1973 1977 1981 1985 1987

Who are the home owners?

Home ownership by social class of head of household

Key

Owner-occupied   Rented from local authority   Rented privately

Professional and managerial

Other non-manual

Skilled manual

Semi-skilled and unskilled

Percentage 0   20   40   60   80   100

provides homes (with some degree of assistance) for elderly and disabled people.

The standard of housing has improved but while most of the old slum areas in cities have been cleared, many of the large square blocks of flats which replaced them as part of the high-rise housing programme of the 1960s have been criticised as being badly designed and built. Many have now been pulled down and replaced with low-rise housing. Big building programmes for some areas in the south of England began towards the end of the 1990s.

Comprehension

Use the information on these two pages to answer the questions.

1 What are the three types of housing mentioned?
2 What is the ratio of houses to flats in Britain?
3 What has happened to home ownership in Britain?
4 What sort of people in the UK are most and least likely to own their houses?
5 Explain the following: 'sheltered' housing, a mortgage, a slum area.

Discussion

Work in pairs.

1 What differences are there between housing in Britain and in your country?
2 What sort of British people are most likely to own their homes? What reasons can you think of?

■ Somewhere to live ■

There are many different types of housing in Britain, ranging from the traditional thatched country cottage to flats in the centre of towns. Houses are often described by the period in which they were built (for example, Georgian, Victorian, 1930s, or post-war) and whether they are terraced, semi-detached or detached. As well as preferring houses to flats, for many people a garden is also an important consideration. Although Britain is relatively small the areas where people live vary considerably: there are new towns and inner cities, suburbs, commuter belts and the open countryside.

Paying for the home you live in is the biggest single item in the budget of most families and getting on the housing 'ladder' can be difficult. First-time house buyers on an average salary may have to borrow 90 or even 100 per cent of the value of the property they want to buy. It is possible for people to borrow up to three times their annual income or sometimes even more. As prices vary, the cost of a six-bedroom farmhouse in a remote part of Scotland is about the same as a small flat in an expensive area of west London. People moving from the north to the south of Britain have to pay a lot more for the same type of house.

The average family moves once every seven years and the process of moving involves an estate agent (responsible for advertising houses for sale), a building society, bank or insurance company for the finance, and a solicitor to handle the legal aspects of the buying and selling. The size of a house or flat in Britain still tends to be measured by the number of bedrooms rather than the area in square metres. In keeping with a nation of home owners, gardening and DIY are popular spare time activities.

A

B

C

- ☐ Victorian terrace
- ☐ 1930s semi-detached house
- ☐ 1960s flats
- ☐ Modern housing estate
- ☐ Old town houses
- ☐ Country cottage
- ☐ Country house

Comprehension

Use the information on these two pages to answer these questions.

1 Match the pictures with the list of house types on page 106.
2 How much do some people borrow to buy a house?
3 What does the text say about the differences in house prices in Britain?
4 How often do people move house? What other people are involved if you want to move house?
5 How is the size of a house still measured in Britain?

Discussion

Work in pairs.

Look at the houses on these two pages. What type of house would you prefer to live in? Give your reasons.

■ New homes ■

Docklands before the new development

When you visit The Lakes you feel you're a thousand miles away. And then you are.

First 15 parties each day get a week's accommodation in the sun free.

A visit to The Lakes is almost like a holiday in itself. In any of the spaciously designed apartments and houses built around a carefully landscaped lake, you feel you could be a thousand miles away. Yet you're a mere ten minutes from Tower Bridge.

And right now it offers exceptional value for money.

1 and 2 bed flats range from £80,000 to £128,000. 3 bed town

homes start at only £345,000. 3 and 4 bed villas from £165,000 to £280,000.

Come and see for yourself. If you're one of the first 15 visiting parties of the day, you'll get a voucher for a week's free accommodation in a four star hotel in Tenerife – for free! So come early.

We're open every day from 10am–5pm. You'll find us at Greenland Dock, Redriff Road, Rotherhithe, London SE16. Tel: 071-237 9007.

Ideal Homes

New housing in Docklands (inset) An advertisement for new Docklands Housing

The need for housing in the south of England has produced new developments in both rural and urban areas. One example of new large-scale building is in the East End of London where fifty years ago London's docklands were the heart of a busy international port. Today most of the ships have gone but the developers, planners, architects and builders have moved in. A new London is being built at high speed. New roads, an airport and a docklands railway have all been built there; houses, flats and offices are being created from the old docks.

While London's skyline changes there are a number of arguments about the direction in which housing should develop. Much of the new Docklands development was designed for people to have easy access to jobs in financial institutions in the City of London, although some local residents have also benefited from the new housing and transport improvements. The speed of the building has meant that environmental planning has not always been possible. Although some of the new buildings have won architectural awards, there has also been criticism of the new architectural styles.

The demand for new homes puts pressure on both city areas and the countryside. Some of the 'Green Belt' of protected land which used to surround London and other towns and cities in southern England is now being used for housing, particularly in areas which have become more affluent.

Homelessness

The number of homeless people in Britain has doubled since 1979. Reasons for this rise include the decline in the availability of rented accommodation (nearly 1 million fewer homes than in 1980), lack of council housing due to government cuts in grants to local authorities, who are responsible for public housing, and the increases in house prices during the 1980s. Unemployment, changes in the social security benefit regulations and the number of young people leaving home also contribute to the problem.

Many local authorities have been forced to put homeless people in hotels and bed-and-breakfast accommodation because of a lack of suitable flats and houses. While real earnings have risen faster than inflation and helped to push up house prices, debt has also increased, helping to leave some of those at the bottom of the scale without a home. One in five families in London are said to live in unsatisfactory conditions and there are an estimated 10,000 people in the capital who have to sleep rough because they have no accommodation at all.

Comprehension

Use the information on these two pages to answer these questions.

1 What changes have occurred in London's docklands and why?
2 Explain the following: developments, planners, Green Belt, sleep rough.
3 Find three factors which contribute to the problem of people without homes.
4 Where do some families without homes live?

Discussion

Work in pairs.

1 Look at the photographs on page 108. Do you think the modern developments are better than the older housing? What sort of architecture do you prefer?
2 Who do you think should be responsible for housing: local government or private industry? What is the system in your country?

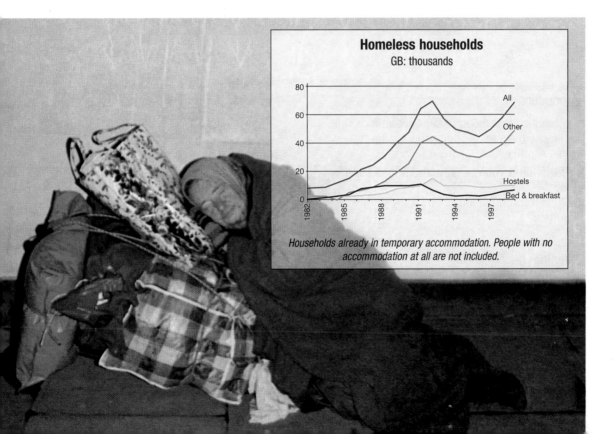

Homeless households
GB: thousands

All
Other
Hostels
Bed & breakfast

Households already in temporary accommodation. People with no accommodation at all are not included.

■ Flats and houses ■

Introduction

In this interview the speaker talks about the house she lives in and the area of London where she lives.

1 How would you describe the house she lives in?
2 Do you think her family own the whole house?

Listening

Listen to the tape and see if you were right. Now answer the following questions.

1 What sort of accommodation does the speaker live in now?
2 Portobello Road and Brixton Market are both street markets. Which one does she live near now?

3 What do you think she means by 'on the latch'?
4 Why does she say 'It's more of a household'?
5 What area did she live in before, and how was it different?
6 Would she like to move back there?

Discussion

Work in pairs.

1 Listen again and list any features of the house and district which you like.
2 Which of these features does the speaker seem to like: street markets, children, young professional couples, expensive cars, narrow streets? Is your own list different?

■ Summary ■

Vocabulary

1 Put the following words and expressions from this unit into groups according to their meaning. Give each group of words a title.

high-rise detached planner flat financial semi-detached tax rented architect rural builder terraced low-rise street developer house mortgage urban cost privately-owned council road cottage

2 Make longer words from the following:
e.g. home: homeless, homelessness
develop terrace architect house environment tradition finance

Expensive waterfront homes in London's Docklands

Discussion

1 What are the main changes that have happened to housing in Britain over the last few years?
2 What type of accommodation do the majority of British people like to live in? Can you think of any reasons?
3 What professions are involved in the buying and selling of houses in your country? Is the system the same as in Britain?
4 Why do you think there are homeless people in Britain? What could be done to improve the situation?

Writing

What sort of a house or flat do you live in? Write a description of it.

14

Transport

■ Public and private transport ■

As in the rest of western Europe, in recent years there has been a large increase in the use of private cars in Britain. By the year 2000 cars, taxis and motorcycles accounted for nearly 85 per cent of all passenger transport in Britain compared with less than 55 per cent in the early 1960s. During the same period travel by bus and coach fell from 25 per cent to 10 per cent of all transport and rail travel fell from 15 per cent to just over 6 per cent. Britain, where the first railways were introduced, now has a declining rail system compared to other European countries: the Germans, the Italians and the French all travel on trains much more than the British. Britain also has the most expensive system of (privatised) rail passenger travel in the European Union.

Following rail privatisation in 1996 passenger rail services are provided by 25 private companies. The organisation of bus and coach transport was also changed and much of it was transferred to the private sector. Smaller buses appeared in towns and cities and there was more competition between companies. As a result of better services and cheaper prices, the number of passengers travelling long distances by bus or coach began to increase again.

Britain started building motorways in the 1960s and there is a sophisticated system of major roads. However, the increase in cars and lorries, particularly in and around London and on the motorways, has caused a number of problems, with more traffic jams and delays for commuters and long-distance travellers.

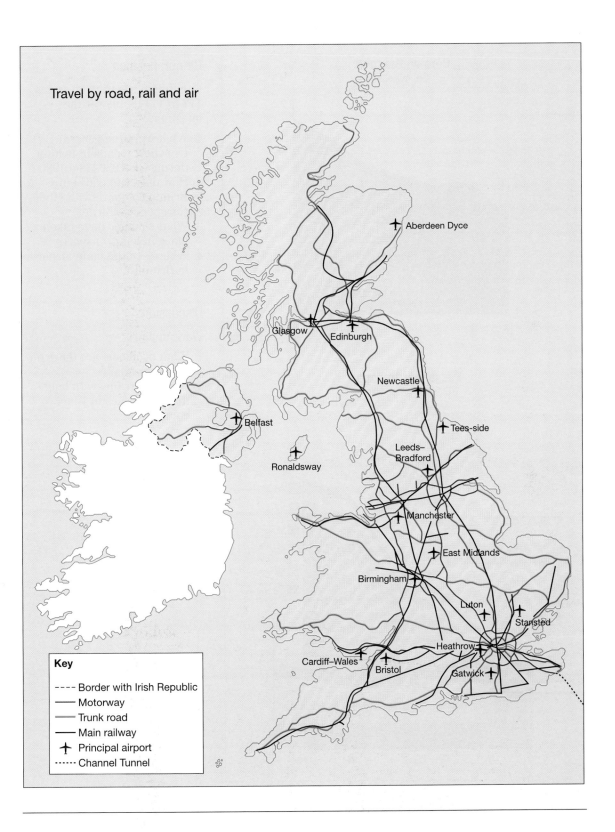

Travel by road, rail and air

Key

- - - - Border with Irish Republic
——— Motorway
——— Trunk road
——— Main railway
✈ Principal airport
· · · · · Channel Tunnel

Aberdeen Dyce
Glasgow
Edinburgh
Newcastle
Tees-side
Belfast
Ronaldsway
Leeds–Bradford
Manchester
East Midlands
Birmingham
Luton
Stansted
Heathrow
Cardiff–Wales
Bristol
Gatwick

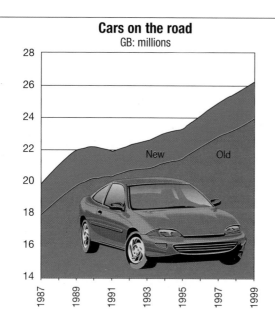

Cars on the road
GB: millions

New   Old

1987 1989 1991 1993 1995 1997 1999

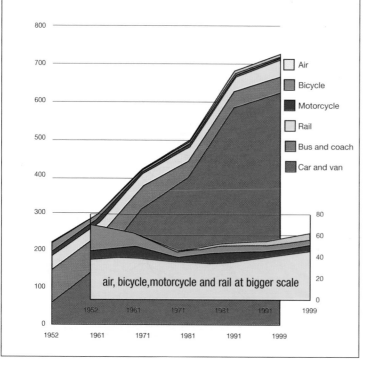

Passenger transport
GB: billion passenger km

- Air
- Bicycle
- Motorcycle
- Rail
- Bus and coach
- Car and van

air, bicycle, motorcycle and rail at bigger scale

1952 1961 1971 1981 1991 1999

Comprehension

Use the information on pages 112 to 114 to answer the questions.

1 What were the general transport trends in Britain during the 1980s and 1990s?
2 How does rail travel in Britain compare with other European countries?
3 What changes have taken place in bus transport?
4 Where are the main airports in Britain?

Discussion

Work in pairs.

1 What problems are there on British roads?
2 Compare trains with long-distance buses in your country.

■ The rise of the car ■

As the number of vehicles on Britain's roads goes up each year other statistics are also affected. For example the percentage of households with two cars rose from 2 per cent in the early 1960s to 23 per cent in 1999, and by the end of the 1980s two-thirds of all journeys to work were made by private transport compared to one-third two decades before. There are more company cars on the roads (usually with only one person in them) and more young people over the age of seventeen are learning to drive and taking driving tests. In general the south-east of England has the highest proportion of households with cars and this also gives the region some of the worst traffic problems. At the moment there are no toll roads in Britain, although such schemes have been considered. In Britain, unlike other European countries, cars drive on the left.

In recent years the British car manufacturing industry – at one time one of the most important in the world – has declined and imports of foreign cars rose from 33 per cent in 1980 to around 50 per cent in 1988.

Despite the increase in traffic British roads are still relatively safe to drive on and the number of serious accidents has fallen over the last decade. Many lives are saved by seat belts which have been compulsory in towns and on the open road since 1983. Demands for

an increase in the maximum speed limit (70 mph/110 kph) have been rejected. A major cause of death and injury on the roads is drinking and driving; the permissible level of alcohol is higher in Britain than in most other European countries.

Heavy traffic on London's orbital motorway, the M25, the longest ring road in the world

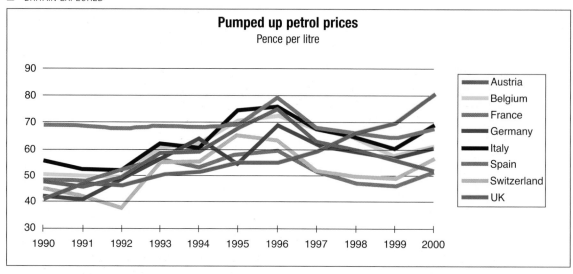

Pumped up petrol prices
Pence per litre

Legend: Austria, Belgium, France, Germany, Italy, Spain, Switzerland, UK

While cars make life more convenient for many people, Britain is beginning to experience some of the difficulties and expense caused by too much traffic. The M25, the London Orbital Motorway and the longest ring road in the world (120 miles/192 km), is a good example. Completed in 1986 at a cost of over £1,000 m, it was designed to reduce traffic problems in the London area but it almost immediately became overcrowded and has since become famous for long traffic jams. The average daily traffic flow rose on all British roads especially on motorways (from 53,000 to 68,000 between 1991 and 1998). At peak times and on some motorways congestion regularly causes serious disruptions.

In London the problems are just as bad and the average speed of the traffic is estimated to be approximately the same as it was at the beginning of the last century. Things are unlikely to improve in the near future. In general, although long-distance journey times have been reduced considerably, the more roads that are built, the more traffic there is to fill them, and the planners' job of predicting the number and type of roads for the future has become extremely difficult. Most of Britain's motorways – including the M25 – were built for lower levels of traffic density and now need constant repairs.

In the future, technology will produce better and more efficient cars but there will be a lot more of them. In Britain, one view of these developments is that in a small area like the UK they will lead to increased concentrations of traffic with problems of parking, traffic jams, pollution and expense. Another view says that the car is a form of personal freedom and that there is no effective acceptable way to control the numbers of vehicles. The debate over the relative merits of public and private transport continues.

Comprehension

Use the information on pages 115 and 116 to answer the questions.

1 Where are some of the worst traffic problems to be found in Britain?
2 Is Britain a safe place to drive in? What reasons for and against this are given?
3 How do UK petrol prices compare with other countries?
4 What and where is the M25?

Discussion

Work in pairs.

1 What is being done to try to improve road transport? Why is this difficult in Britain?
2 Where are the worst traffic problems to be found in your country? What measures are taken to reduce the problems?
3 What can be done to help protect the environment from the effects of road traffic?

■ By rail ■

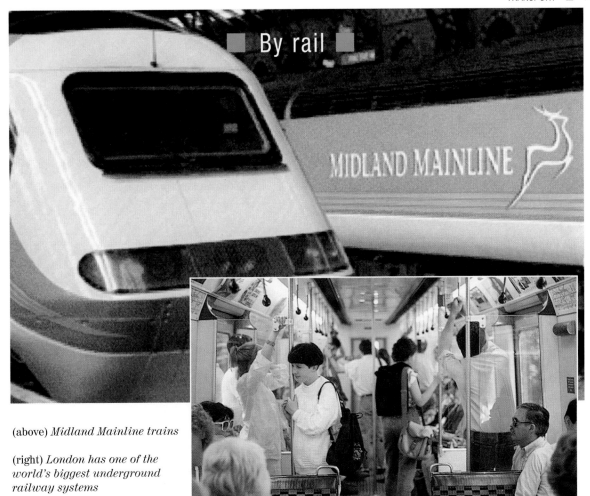

(above) *Midland Mainline trains*

(right) *London has one of the world's biggest underground railway systems*

Britain has a modern rail system and work has been done to improve the networks (e.g. electrification of some main lines). In London underground stations have been renovated and new lines built and there are plans to modernise the whole system with a combination of public and private money. New railway systems in Glasgow and Newcastle were built during the 1980s and the London Docklands Railway was completed in 1987. In some cities trams have begun to reappear as a form of public transport.

However, rail privatisation in 1996 caused a number of problems and travelling by train on the mainline railways is expensive: for example, the journey from London to Edinburgh (600 km) takes only four hours but the standard single fare costs the equivalent of six months' car road tax. Despite a complicated system of reduced fares for students, families, old people, and those who can travel at certain times and on certain days, rail fares cannot compete with the cheaper long-distance coaches. Much to the irritation of commuters and passengers fares have consistently risen by more than the annual rate of inflation and some people argue that less government support for the railways (the lowest level of subsidy in Western Europe) inevitably means higher fares. There are also complaints about trains being late and overcrowded but despite this the number of passengers travelling by train began to increase again towards the end of the 1990s. During this period the number of people using the London tube almost doubled. Around 850.000 commuters travel daily into London and use the tube.

■ By air and sea ■

(above) *Jumbo jets at London's Gatwick Airport*

(left) *London's Heathrow Airport – Terminal 4*

London's Heathrow Airport is the busiest international airport in the world and British Airways is one of the largest airlines. During the 1980s the airline flew to destinations in seventy-two countries and annually carried more than 18 million passengers. It was privatised in 1986. Heathrow Airport's four terminals now handle nearly 70 million passengers a year and London has four other airports, including Gatwick, all of which handle international flights. The number of people travelling by air both for business and pleasure is growing and traffic at all airports in Britain increased rapidly during the 1990s.

TOP TEN EUROPEAN AIRPORTS World ranking and total passengers in 1999		
4	London Heathrow	62,263,365
7	Frankfurt	45,838,864
8	Paris Charles de Gaulle	43,597,194
11	Amsterdam	36,772,015
21	London Gatwick	30,559,227
25	Madrid	27,994,193
32	Paris Orly	25,349,112
33	Rome	24,029,326
40	Munich	21,282,906
41	Zurich	20,875,311

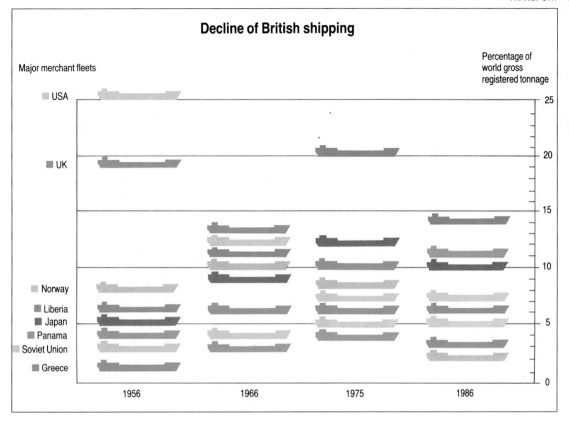

Decline of British shipping

Major merchant fleets

Percentage of
world gross
registered tonnage

- USA
- UK
- Norway
- Liberia
- Japan
- Panama
- Soviet Union
- Greece

25
20
15
10
5
0

1956   1966   1975   1986

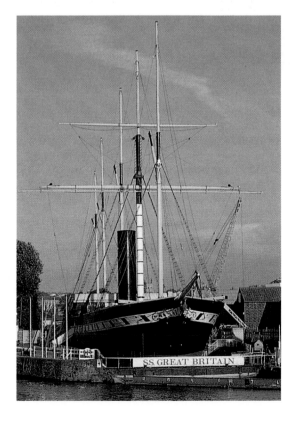

The SS Great Britain, *now on display in Bristol*

Comprehension

Use the information on pages 117 to 119 to answer the questions.

1 Which areas of British transport have increased and decreased?
2 Can you find any reasons why rail travel is expensive in Britain?
3 How is it possible to get a reduced fare on the railways?
4 Look back to page 50. How has air traffic changed?
5 Describe the decline of Britain's shipping.

Discussion

Work in pairs.

1 How have transport changes affected London?
2 Which method of transport do you prefer and why?

■ One man and his cars ■

Introduction

1 What sort of work do you think the speaker does?
2 How would you describe his car?
3 Do you think he looks after it?

Listening

Listen and see if you were right.
Now answer these questions.

1 What two jobs does the speaker have?
2 When did he first get a driving licence?
3 How much driving does he do each week? What sort of driving is it?
4 How many vehicles does he have? What does he use them for?

5 How does he treat his car?
6 What's the difference between the car he used to have and the car he has now?
7 What does he say about British car manufacturing?

Discussion

Work in pairs.

1 Listen for these words and match them with their definitions: crossbred, charisma, kudos.
    a status b personality c mixture
2 Do you agree with the speaker's view of Japanese and British cars?

■ Summary ■

Vocabulary

1 Put the list of words under the following headings: Road; Rail; Sea; Air.

car ship underground airport licence truck subsidy ring road international jam train fare boat coach carriage inter-city commuter terminal motorway cargo parking aeroplane electrification tube flight airline tunnel

2 Add another word to each of the following to make an expression used in this unit.

e.g. ring: ring road

company speed toll reduced driving public seat long

Discussion

1 What are the differences between transport in your country and in Britain?
2 Why do you think the car has become so important in Britain?

3 It is sometimes said that there are only three possible ways of dealing with increasing traffic:
a ignore it
b build more roads
c encourage other forms of transport.
Which method has Britain chosen to adopt? Can you think of any other possibilities?
4 How do you think transport should be paid for? What are your views on public and private transport?
5 Make a list of as many different forms of transport as possible; which ones do you use? What are the various advantages and disadvantages?

Writing

Prepare questions on how people in your class travel to school or work. Collect the answers and report your findings.

London buses

Health

■ The National Health Service ■

The British National Health Service (NHS) was set up in 1948 and was designed to provide equal basic health care, free of charge, for everybody in the country. Before this time health care had to be paid for by individuals.

Nowadays central government is directly responsible for the NHS although it is administered by local health authorities. About 83 per cent of the cost of the health service is paid for by general taxation and the rest is met from the National Insurance contributions paid by those in work. There are charges for prescriptions and dental care but many people, such as children, pregnant women, pensioners, and those on Income Support, are exempt from payment.

Most people are registered with a local doctor (a GP, or General Practitioner) who is increasingly likely to be part of a health centre which serves the community.

As the population of Britain gets older, the hospital service now treats more patients than ever before, although patients spend less time in hospital. NHS hospitals – many of which were built in the nineteenth century – provide nearly half a million beds and have over 480,000 medical staff. The NHS is the biggest employer in Europe although Britain actually spends less per person on health care than most of her European neighbours.

During the 1980s there was considerable restructuring of the Health Service with an increased emphasis on managerial efficiency and the privatisation of some services (for example, cleaning). In the 1990s a number of NHS reforms were introduced by the Conservative and Labour governments including self-management of hospitals and a 'market' for patients who were referred to hospitals for treatment. Hospitals and GPs were given more financial responsibility. The political questions continue about how the NHS should be run, how much money should be provided to support it and where the money should come from.

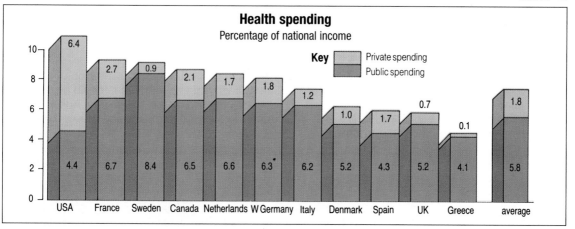

Health spending
Percentage of national income

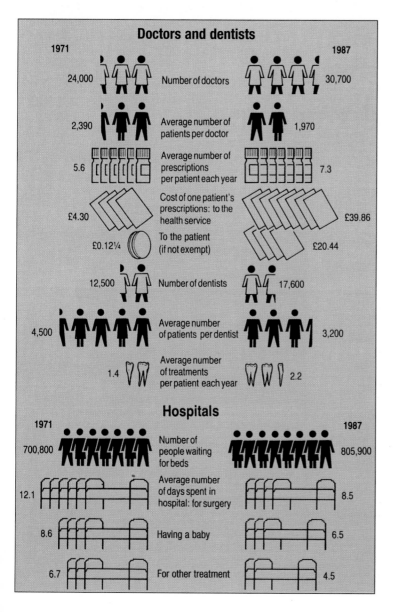

Comprehension

Use the information on these two pages to answer the questions.

1 What was the original aim of the National Health Service and what used to happen before it began?
2 How is the NHS paid for?
3 What reforms have taken place in the NHS?
4 How does health care expenditure in Britain compare with other countries?

Discussion

Work in pairs.

1 Is there any evidence that medical and dental services are improving?
2 What are the advantages of free medical care?

■ How healthy are the British? ■

It is difficult to judge exactly how healthy a nation is but there are various indicators such as how long people live and whether there are still many common serious infectious diseases. In general, compared with fifty years ago, the health of people in Britain has improved considerably, partly as a result of better housing and education, and a higher standard of living.

However, not everybody enjoys a standard of health consistent with living in one of the world's top industrial nations. Health and health care vary considerably from area to area and middle-class people tend to enjoy better health than working-class people. Unemployment, poverty, poor housing and bad diet are still major contributors to poor health. On the one hand, as people live in better conditions, eat better food and take more exercise, health standards tend to rise and people live longer. But there are other health problems such as smoking-related diseases, alcoholism and drug abuse, the spread of AIDs, and the number of people who die from cancer.

One worrying feature about health in Britain is that more people die of heart disease and strokes (40 per cent of men and 38 per cent of women) than of any other group of diseases. Heart disease kills about 30,000 men under the age of 65 every year.

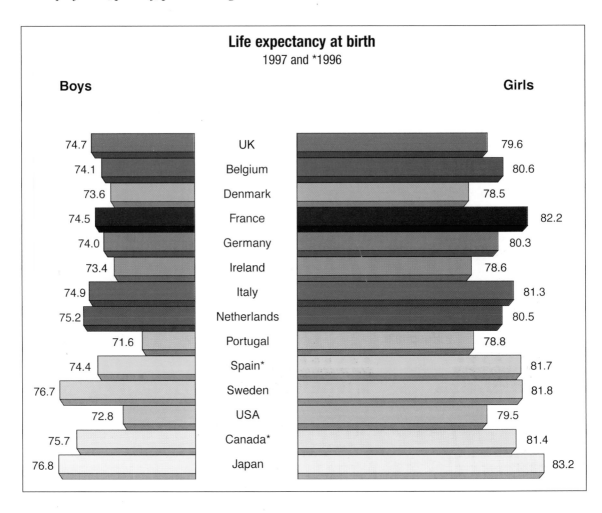

Life expectancy at birth
1997 and *1996

Boys		Girls
74.7	UK	79.6
74.1	Belgium	80.6
73.6	Denmark	78.5
74.5	France	82.2
74.0	Germany	80.3
73.4	Ireland	78.6
74.9	Italy	81.3
75.2	Netherlands	80.5
71.6	Portugal	78.8
74.4	Spain*	81.7
76.7	Sweden	81.8
72.8	USA	79.5
75.7	Canada*	81.4
76.8	Japan	83.2

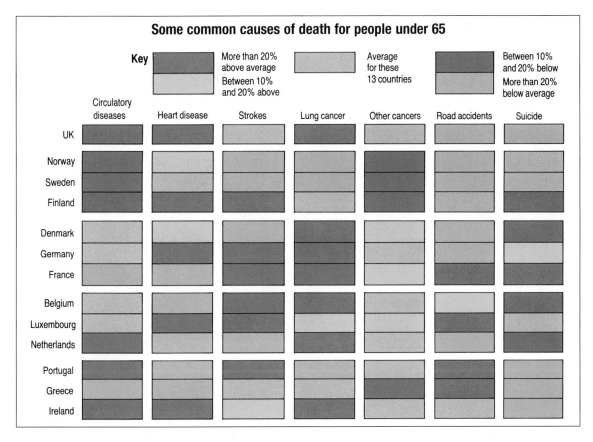

Some common causes of death for people under 65

Rates in Britain are among the highest in the world and have increased over the last ten years. Most victims have a history of high cholesterol levels, high blood pressure, or smoking, and attempts have been made to improve the British diet and to persuade people to stop smoking. Between 1972 and 1999 the percentage of male smokers fell from 52 to 28 per cent; for women the figure fell from 42 to 26 per cent. Efforts have been made to improve co-ordination between government departments to influence the nation's diet and to advise on food production and consumption.

Comprehension

Use the information on these two pages to answer the questions.

1 What indicators can be used to measure the health of a nation?
2 What factors contribute to good health? Which ones contribute to poor health?
3 How long do people live in Britain compared to other countries?
4 What major health problems remain in Britain?

Discussion

Work in pairs.

1 What sort of activities do people do in your country to stay healthy? What do you do?
2 Do people smoke a lot in your country? Has the government done anything to reduce smoking?

■ A healthy diet ■

Although the British diet has changed over the last few years not all the changes have been for the better. For example, people now eat more convenience food (e.g. frozen products) and fast food (e.g. hamburgers) than they used to. Medical advice suggests that people should have a balanced diet that contains more fresh fruit, vegetables and fibre, and less sugar and fat. Smoking and drinking less is also recommended.

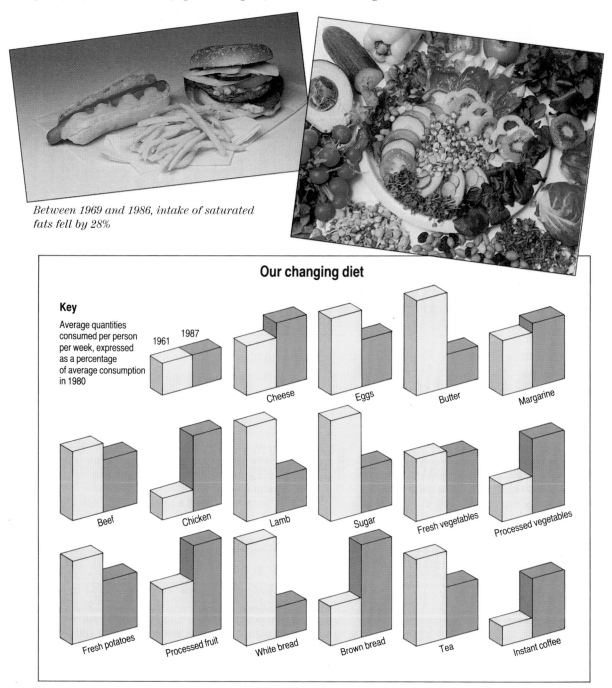

Between 1969 and 1986, intake of saturated fats fell by 28%

Our changing diet

Key

Average quantities consumed per person per week, expressed as a percentage of average consumption in 1980

1961 1987

Cheese · Eggs · Butter · Margarine · Beef · Chicken · Lamb · Sugar · Fresh vegetables · Processed vegetables · Fresh potatoes · Processed fruit · White bread · Brown bread · Tea · Instant coffee

■ The debate over public v private ■

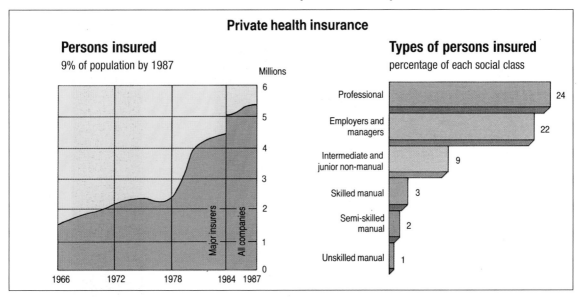

Private health insurance

Persons insured

9% of population by 1987

Types of persons insured

percentage of each social class

The number of people covered by private medical insurance rose from 1.6 million in the late 1960s to over 5.5 million, around 10 per cent of the population, by the late 1980s. Other people decide to 'go private' in order to pay for a particular operation (perhaps one for which they might have to wait for a long time under the NHS). Most private treatment involves a small range of surgical operations and the private sector does not provide emergency treatment or care for those who are ill for long periods. Most of the 10,000 private hospital beds are in private hospitals, although there are some private beds in NHS hospitals as well. Some NHS staff work in both the public and private sector; nearly all the medical staff in both public and private hospitals were originally trained by the NHS.

The view of the Conservative government during the 1980s was that people should be given the freedom of choice to pay for their own medical care if they wish, and that the National Health Service must become more efficient and more cost-effective. Prescription charges rose and elements of privatisation included the introduction of charges for eyesight checks and increases in dental treatment charges on the grounds that many people could afford them and should therefore pay. Opponents said that many people would

not be able to pay and that health standards would decline as a result. Figures for private health insurance have changed little since the end of the 1980s.

Comprehension

Use the information on these two pages to answer the questions.

1 What advice do doctors give British people about their diet?
2 Find five examples of how the British diet has changed.
3 What sort of treatment is mainly undertaken by private hospitals? What kind of activities do they not undertake?
4 Which NHS charges increased during the 1980s?

Discussion

Work in pairs.

1 What do you think constitutes a 'healthy' diet? How healthy do you consider your own diet to be?
2 Do you have to pay for medical and dental treatment in your country?

■ A doctor's view ■

Introduction

1 Match the definitions with the medical expressions:
   a a hospital with a medical school
   b a doctor's work, or place of work
   c a doctor who treats all types of illness
   d a specialist doctor
   e someone who visits a hospital for treatment but does not stay overnight
      1 consultant
      2 General Practitioner
      3 outpatient
      4 teaching hospital
      5 practice

2 In your country, can you choose the doctor or hospital you go to? Does the choice vary from place to place?

Listening

1 When did the speaker qualify as a doctor?
2 When did she begin to feel that there were certain things wrong with the medical service?

3 In what sense can patients 'vote with their feet'?
4 Why is this more difficult in small communities?
5 What are the two advantages to the patient of living in a big city like London?
6 How long might a patient have to wait
   a for a hospital appointment in a small town?
   b for an outpatient appointment?
   c in the waiting room after arriving for an appointment?
7 What is the difference in attitude between people who travel to get private medicine, and those who travel to get NHS treatment?

Discussion

Work in pairs.

1 Why does the speaker think people 'feel better' simply as a result of choosing private medicine?
2 Summarise the inequalities in medical treatment mentioned by the speaker.

■ Summary ■

Vocabulary

1 Give a definition for each of these words or expressions:

GP   nurse   dentist   prescription   doctor
hospital   diet   heart disease   fast food
smoker   alcoholism   insurance
health centre   ward   infectious disease
patient   convenience food   fat

2 Make an adjective from each of the following nouns:

health   convenience   infection
poverty   finance   Europe   origin
industry

Discussion

1 What major problems does the NHS in Britain face?
2 What is your opinion on the question of public health care versus private medicine? What is the best way of funding health care?
3 Do you think people are more healthy in your country than they used to be? What has changed?
4 Have you had any experience of British food? If so what is your opinion of it?

Writing

Imagine you have been asked to plan a week's menu for healthy eating. Write a menu for five days, with three meals each day (breakfast, lunch, dinner). Compare menus with other students.

A night nurse on duty in a hospital ward

16

Leisure

■ Spare time ■

British people now have more free time and holidays than they did thirty years ago. The average number of working hours has fallen, and by the mid-1990s almost all full-time manual employees were entitled to four weeks' holiday or more, in addition to public holidays including Christmas and Easter. Although for some people there was more leisure time (for the increasing number of pensioners for example), in general the pace of life became busier in Britain in the 1990s.

Typical popular pastimes in the UK include shopping, listening to pop music, going to pubs, playing and watching sport, going on holidays, doing outdoor activities and watching TV. The number of people playing sports has risen, partly due to the availability of more sporting facilities such as local leisure centres. As more people become aware of the necessity for exercise, it is estimated that one third of the adult population regularly takes part in outdoor sport and about a quarter in indoor sport. Among the most popular sporting activities are walking, swimming, snooker and darts; fishing is the most popular country sport. Football, cricket, horse racing and motor sports are all popular spectator sports. Many magazines are published which relate to popular and minority sports and interests.

Multi-screen cinemas have become more common and the number of people going to the cinema increased in the mid-1980s, having fallen by more than a half between 1971 and 1984. This was despite a large increase in the popularity of home videos: Britain has one of the highest rates of home video ownership in the world.

Pubs are an important part of British social life (more than restaurants) and more money is spent on drinking than on any other form of leisure activity. Holidays are the next major leisure cost, followed by television, radio, musical instruments, and eating out.

If they have enough money, people travel more, usually by car or by air, and they take more holidays. The numbers going abroad increased from 7 million in the early 1970s to 32 million in the late 1990s, with Spain still the most popular foreign destination.

Major UK National Holidays

New Year Holiday	January 1st
Good Friday	March/April
Easter Monday	March/April
May Day Holiday	May
Spring Holiday	May
Summer Holiday	August
Christmas Day	December 25th
Boxing Day	December 26th

Note: The exact date of some holidays (e.g. Easter) varies each year. Scotland and Northern Ireland have some different national holidays.

Killing time

Key Average hours spent each week on:

- Employment and travel
- Essential activities
- Sleep
- Free time

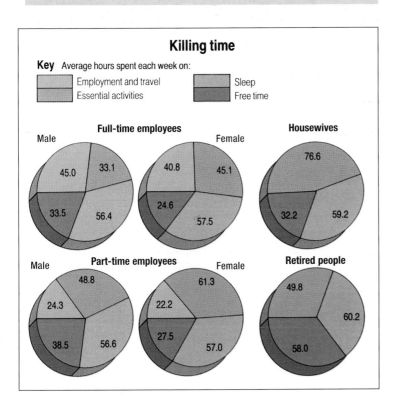

Full-time employees
Male: 45.0, 33.1, 33.5, 56.4
Female: 40.8, 45.1, 24.6, 57.5

Housewives
76.6, 32.2, 59.2

Part-time employees
Male: 48.8, 24.3, 38.5, 56.6
Female: 61.3, 22.2, 27.5, 57.0

Retired people
49.8, 60.2, 58.0

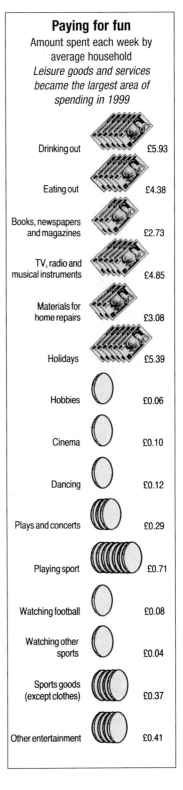

Paying for fun

Amount spent each week by average household
Leisure goods and services became the largest area of spending in 1999

Drinking out	£5.93
Eating out	£4.38
Books, newspapers and magazines	£2.73
TV, radio and musical instruments	£4.85
Materials for home repairs	£3.08
Holidays	£5.39
Hobbies	£0.06
Cinema	£0.10
Dancing	£0.12
Plays and concerts	£0.29
Playing sport	£0.71
Watching football	£0.08
Watching other sports	£0.04
Sports goods (except clothes)	£0.37
Other entertainment	£0.41

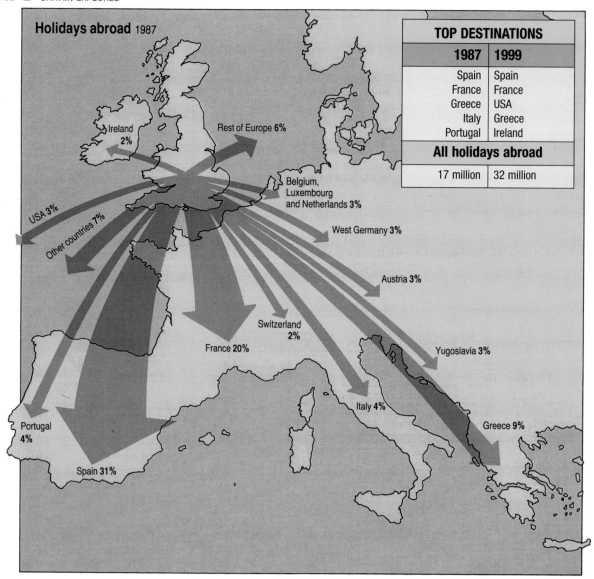

Holidays abroad 1987

Ireland 2%

Rest of Europe 6%

Belgium, Luxembourg and Netherlands 3%

USA 3%

Other countries 7%

West Germany 3%

Austria 3%

Switzerland 2%

France 20%

Yugoslavia 3%

Portugal 4%

Italy 4%

Greece 9%

Spain 31%

TOP DESTINATIONS	
1987	**1999**
Spain	Spain
France	France
Greece	USA
Italy	Greece
Portugal	Ireland
All holidays abroad	
17 million	32 million

Comprehension

Use the information on pages 130 to 132 to answer the questions.

1 What free time and holidays do people in Britain have?
2 Why has sport become more popular?
3 How has cinema-going changed in recent years? What has helped to cause these changes?
4 What are the most popular leisure activities in Britain?
5 Which are the most popular destinations for British people going abroad on holiday?

Discussion

Work in pairs.

1 Do people have more spare time than they used to in your country? When are the major public holidays?
2 What leisure activities do you prefer? How much time and money do you spend on them?

■ Sport ■

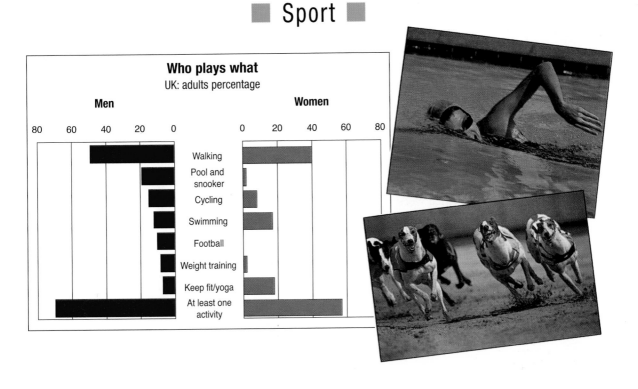

Who plays what
UK: adults percentage

	Men					Women			
80	60	40	20	0	0	20	40	60	80

- Walking
- Pool and snooker
- Cycling
- Swimming
- Football
- Weight training
- Keep fit/yoga
- At least one activity

Gambling

Britain introduced a National Lottery in 1994 and this has proved to be extremely popular. An estimated 80 per cent of the adult population play the lottery, each spending a weekly average of £2.50. Horse racing is also one of the biggest attractions, particularly for famous races such as The Grand National and The Derby. Betting shops ('bookmakers') can be found in most high streets. Dog racing is also popular in some parts of the country.

Other forms of gambling include amusement arcades and pub games, casinos, bingo, and the weekly football pools where very large prizes of a million pounds or more can be won. It has been estimated that over 90 per cent of adults gamble at some time or other with about 40 per cent gambling regularly.

Comprehension

Use the information on this page to answer the questions.

1 Match the sports shown in the photographs with the correct names.
2 Which sports are played more by women than men?
3 What are the most popular sports in Britain?
4 What examples are given of types of gambling?

Discussion

Work in pairs.

1 Of the sports mentioned which ones are your favourites?
2 Do you think gambling is a harmless activity or not? Do you gamble?

■ How people relax ■

Pubs and clubs

Going to pubs is a very popular leisure-time activity. In a recent survey seven out of ten adults said they went to pubs, one third of them once a week or more often.

Types of pubs vary considerably from quiet, rural establishments with traditional games, such as skittles and dominoes, to city pubs where different sorts of entertainment such as drama and live music can often be found. The opening hours of pubs, which were previously strictly controlled, have been relaxed and many pubs now serve food as well as drink.

Some pubs have become more welcoming to families with younger children than in the past, although children under fourteen are still not allowed in the bar.

British drinking habits have changed with lager and continental beers now more popular than traditional forms of British beer. In cities, wine bars have appeared in competition with pubs. Although, in general, people in Britain now drink more than they used to, new types of drinks such as alcohol-free beer and wine have appeared and there has been a general move to educate people more about the dangers of drinking too much.

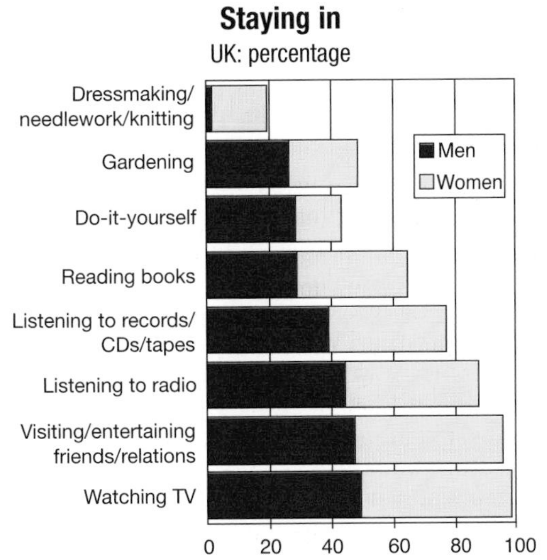
Staying in
UK: percentage
Dressmaking/needlework/knitting
Gardening
Do-it-yourself
Reading books
Listening to records/CDs/tapes
Listening to radio
Visiting/entertaining friends/relations
Watching TV
Men
Women
0
20
40
60
80
100

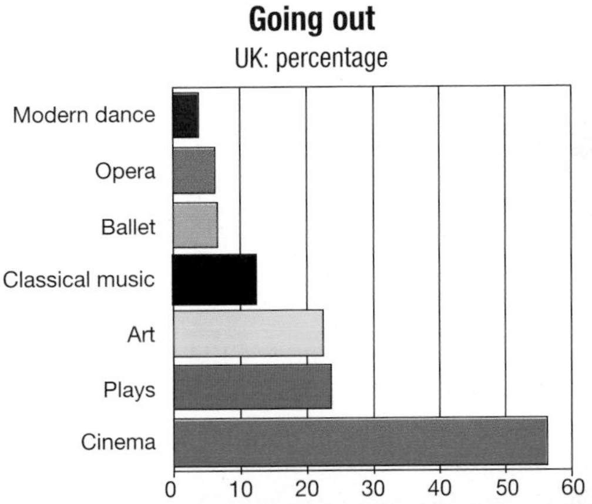
Going out
UK: percentage
Modern dance
Opera
Ballet
Classical music
Art
Plays
Cinema
0
10
20
30
40
50
60

FRESH FRUIT

Reading

Despite the increase in TV watching, reading is still an important leisure activity in Britain and there is a very large number of magazines and books published on a wide variety of subjects. The biggest-selling magazines in Britain (after the TV guides which sell over 3 million copies a week) are women's and pop music publications.

The best-selling books are not great works of literature but stories of mystery and romance which sell in huge quantities (Agatha Christie's novels, for example, have sold more than 300 million copies). It has been estimated that only about 3 per cent of the population read 'classics' such as Charles Dickens or Jane Austen, whereas the figures for popular book sales can be enormous, particularly if the books are connected with TV shows or dramatisations.

Comprehension

Use the information on pages 134 to 137 to answer the questions.

1 Find four examples of popular leisure-time activities.
2 How have pubs and drinking habits in Britain changed in recent years?
3 What are the most popular types of magazines in Britain?
4 What sort of books do people in Britain like reading most?

Discussion

Work in pairs.

1 What are your favourite sorts of books and magazines?
2 Do you agree with the view that television is gradually replacing reading?

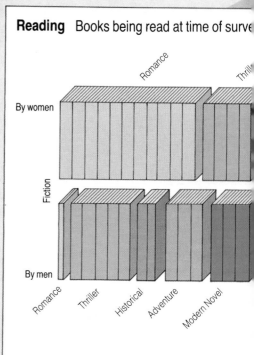

Reading Books being read at time of surve

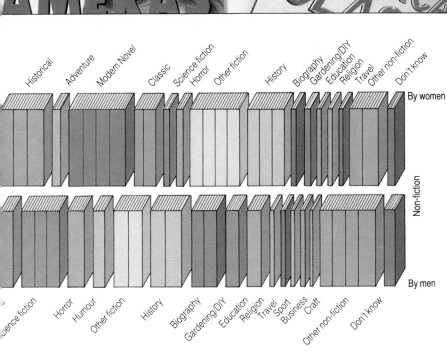

Historical
Adventure
Modern Novel
Classic
Science fiction
Horror
Other fiction
History
Biography
Gardening/DIY
Education
Religion
Travel
Other non-fiction
Don't know

By women

Non-fiction

By men

Science fiction
Horror
Humour
Other fiction
History
Biography
Gardening/DIY
Education
Religion
Travel
Sport
Business
Craft
Other non-fiction
Don't know

■ On stage ■

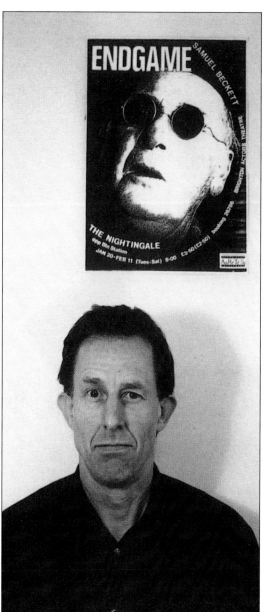

Introduction

David Lavender is Artistic Director of the Komedia Theatre, Brighton. Here he is considering the question of why very few people go to the theatre in Britain.

1 What sort of people go to the theatre in your country?
2 Do you ever go to the theatre? Why? (Why not?)
3 How can experiences at school affect people's attitude to the theatre?

Listening

1 Which media does the speaker say are in competition with the theatre?
2 Which classes of people go to the theatre in Britain?
3 How have audiences changed since Shakespeare's time?
4 Why can people easily be put off theatre-going?
5 How does the education system affect people's attitude towards Shakespeare?
6 How is this relevant to people's attitude to theatre in general?
7 What can turn people into lifelong theatre-goers?
8 When did theatre begin to change in Britain? How?

Discussion

Work in pairs.

1 Why do you think the speaker works in the theatre?
2 What is your own experience of studying or seeing plays in English? 'A bore' or 'a positive experience'?

■ Summary ■

Vocabulary

Look at this list of leisure activities. How much time do you spend on each of them during a week? Put them in order starting with the one you spend most time on.

    playing sport   going to the cinema
    going to the theatre   watching TV
    reading books   reading magazines
    outdoor activities   listening to music

Discussion

1 What sport do you most like watching?
2 Which magazine do you read most often?
3 What's the best film you've seen this year?
4 How much time do you spend watching TV?

Writing

Prepare some more questions and then ask as many other people in your class as possible to give you their answers. Report your results.

The Media

■ Newspapers ■

More daily newspapers are sold per person in the UK than in almost any other country: there are twelve national daily newspapers and eleven national Sunday ones. While the more serious newspapers have a lot of home and international news, some of the more popular 'tabloids' (so called because of their size) concentrate on the more spectacular and scandalous aspects of life in Britain.

Although newspaper sales have fallen slightly over the past few years, newspapers have an important effect on public opinion. Most British newspapers are owned by big businesses and although they are not directly linked to political parties, there are strong connections. The majority of newspapers – even those which carry little serious news – are conservative in outlook.

The old image of London's Fleet Street as the centre of the newspaper printing and publishing world has changed, and in fact all the big newspapers have moved from Fleet Street to more modern premises. New technology has altered the whole shape of the industry, with changes in the production process and a reduction in the number of employees.

One of the beneficial results of computerised production has been improved graphics and photographs, a development first seen in The *Independent*, founded in 1986 and Britain's first new quality newspaper since the last century. The tendency has been for newspapers to become smaller but to contain more pages. Sunday papers have colour magazines and several of the dailies have weekend supplements, perhaps because people now have more time to read them. Competition for circulation is intense and newspapers have tried several methods to increase the number of people who read them, including the use of colour, competitions and national bingo games. Running a newspaper is an expensive and competitive business and several new papers started and failed during the 1980s. Overall, the number of people reading newspapers has declined in recent years.

MAJOR REGIONAL PAPERS
Scotland
Sunday Post
Sunday Mail
Daily Record
England
London Evening Standard
Manchester Evening News
Wolverhampton Express and Star
Liverpool Echo
Yorkshire Post
Wales
Western Mail

Newspaper sales
July 2000: millions

National dailies

Quality papers

	millions
Daily Telegraph	1.02
The Times	0.72
Financial Times	0.45
Guardian	0.39
Independent	0.22

Popular papers

	millions
Sun	3.59
Daily Mail	2.42
Mirror	2.30
Daily Express	1.03
Daily Star	0.63

National Sundays

Quality papers

	millions
Sunday Times	1.31
Sunday Telegraph	0.80
Observer	0.43
Independent on Sunday	0.24

Popular papers

	millions
News of the World	4.02
Mail on Sunday	2.32
Sunday Mirror	1.93
Sunday People	1.51
Sunday Express	0.95

Comprehension

Use the information on these two pages to answer the questions.

1 Explain the following: daily, quality, national, local, popular.
2 Which national newspapers sell the most copies?
3 How has the newspaper business changed in recent years?
4 What other sorts of newspapers are there in addition to national ones?

Discussion

Work in pairs.

1 Make a list of the things you would expect to find in a newspaper. Which give information and which provide entertainment?
2 How do newspapers affect the way people think?

■ Radio ■

BBC Radio broadcasts five national services to the United Kingdom plus regional services in Wales (including programmes in Welsh), Scotland and Northern Ireland. These are:

Radio 1: pop and rock music;
Radio 2: light music, entertainment and sport;
Radio 3: classical music, drama and documentaries;
Radio 4: news, documentaries, drama and entertainment and educational programmes for schools and adults;
Radio 5: sport, educational programmes and children's programmes.

There are also thirty-two BBC Local Radio stations and a number of independent local stations. The first national commercial radio licences were issued in 1992 and many radio stations now also broadcast on the internet. There is advertising on the independent commercial channels.

The External Service of the BBC broadcasts over 700 hours of programmes a week in thirty-seven languages, including the English-language World Service and BBC English by Radio and Television. It is estimated that over 120 million people listen to the service.

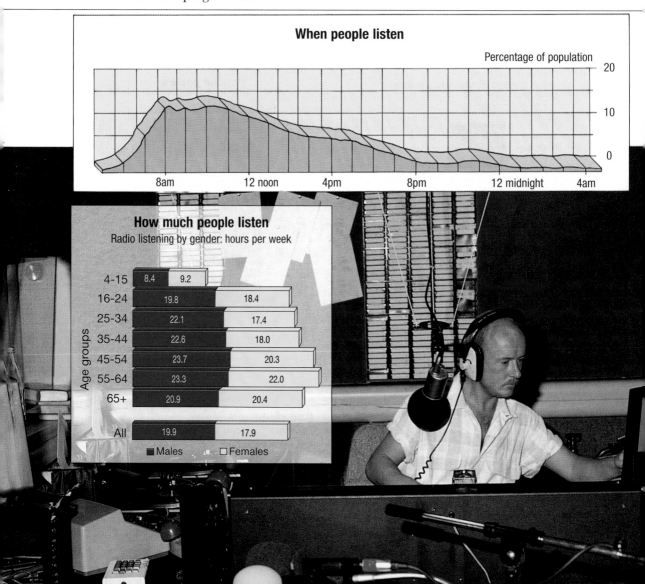

When people listen

Percentage of population

20

10

0

8am   12 noon   4pm   8pm   12 midnight   4am

How much people listen
Radio listening by gender: hours per week

Age groups	Males	Females
4-15	8.4	9.2
16-24	19.8	18.4
25-34	22.1	17.4
35-44	22.6	18.0
45-54	23.7	20.3
55-64	23.3	22.0
65+	20.9	20.4
All	19.9	17.9

■ Males   □ Females

■ The internet ■

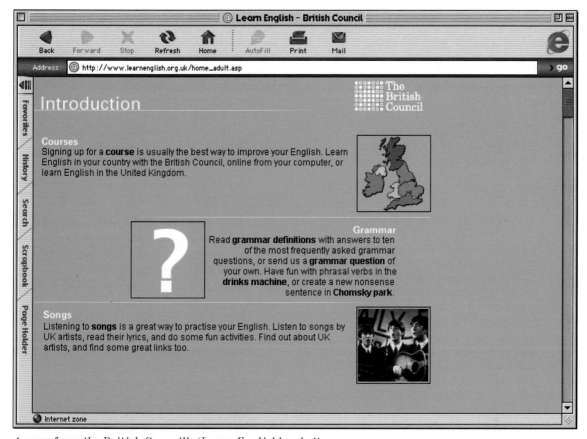

A page from the British Council's 'Learn English' website

By the end of the 1990s the internet and world-wide web had become increasingly important as a contributor to education, entertainment and information. By the year 2000 38 per cent of all households in Britain owned a computer and 86 per cent of primary schools and 98 per cent of secondary schools were connected to the internet. In 2000 over a third of all people in Britain used e-mail. With rapid developments in technology the figures for use at home, in school and at work will continue to rise. The internet is already critical to almost all areas of business and communication.

Comprehension

Use the information on these two pages to answer the questions.

1 What are the main differences between BBC Radios 1, 2, 3, 4 and 5?
2 Why is the BBC External Service important?
3 Is there any advertising on radio in Britain?
4 What can you now do, via the internet, that was not possible before?

Discussion

Work in pairs.

1 Do you listen to the radio? What sort of programmes do you prefer?
2 What difference has the internet made to you?

■ Television ■

By the end of the 1990s there were five channels on British TV: BBC1 and BBC2 plus three independent channels: ITV, Channel 4 and Channel 5. Independent channels get their income from advertisements but there is no advertising on the BBC channels: instead the BBC's revenue comes from licence fees, payable by everybody who has a television, plus some additional funds from Parliament. Both the BBC and ITV sell programmes overseas which adds to their revenue.

The BBC is incorporated under a Royal Charter, which means it is a state organisation but not government controlled. The first television broadcasts began in 1936. The Independent Television Authority was created by Act of Parliament in 1954 to provide an additional television broadcasting service. Commercial television consists of fifteen ITV programme companies providing programmes in fourteen different regions. An increasing number of programmes are now made by independent production companies. A second BBC channel (BBC2) began broadcasting in 1964. A second commercial channel (Channel 4) started in 1982 and a third (Channel 5) in 1997.

Channels are generally expected to provide programmes which do not overlap with other channel's productions and there is a Broadcasting Standards Council which is designed to make sure that unsuitable programmes are not shown.

By the end of the 1980s the total number of UK TV licences was around 19 million, of which 2.5 million were for black and white sets and 16.5 million for colour. During the 1980s and 1990s cable and satellite TV both played an increasing role in the media in Britain, providing a greater choice for those prepared to pay for it.

In the future, digital technology and market forces offer new possibilities and the likelihood of further deregulation and commercialisation of TV.

Who watches what?

One of the biggest changes in the way people in Britain have spent their leisure time in recent years has been the increase in the amount of time spent watching television. The average winter viewing figures are now about twenty-eight hours per week.

As you might expect, television viewing is less popular in summer than in winter and more popular with old people than with any other age group. Viewing also varies according to social class, with professional

(above) *A modern TV set*
(below) *Watching TV in the 1930s*

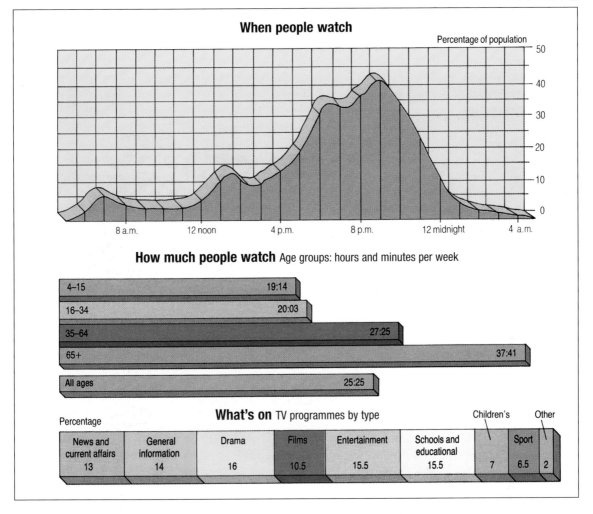

When people watch

Percentage of population

8 a.m. 12 noon 4 p.m. 8 p.m. 12 midnight 4 a.m.

How much people watch Age groups: hours and minutes per week

Age	hours and minutes
4–15	19:14
16–34	20:03
35–64	27:25
65+	37:41
All ages	25:25

What's on TV programmes by type

Percentage

News and current affairs	General information	Drama	Films	Entertainment	Schools and educational	Children's	Sport	Other
13	14	16	10.5	15.5	15.5	7	6.5	2

and managerial classes watching less than the unskilled and the unemployed. On average, women watch more than men.

British TV has an international reputation for producing programmes of a high quality such as documentaries, nature programmes, comedies and drama series and according to the government there should be a combination of 'competition, quality and choice' in any plans for the future of TV. However, not everyone agrees that more TV means better TV and it has been argued that the standard of programmes may drop in the future with companies concentrating on making programmes with a mass appeal such as soap operas, quiz shows and situation comedies. 'Minority' programmes, such as many of those broadcast on BBC2 and Channel 4, might disappear.

Comprehension

Use the information on these two pages to answer the questions.

1 Who watches the most TV in Britain? How much do they watch?
2 How is TV paid for in Britain?
3 What sort of programmes are the most common according to the figures?

Discussion

Work in pairs.

1 What are 'minority' programmes? What do some people think may happen to these programmes in the future?
2 Do you think there should be censorship of TV programmes?

■ TV or not TV? ■

Introduction

1 How much television do you watch in a week?
2 What sort of programmes do you like best?
3 Do you think there is a maximum amount of time that people should watch television?

Listening

1 When does the speaker watch television?
2 Which programmes does he like?
3 When does his daughter watch television?
4 What examples does he give of programmes that are good for children?

5 What does he see as the two main dangers to children?
6 Does he feel that the number of hours you watch is important?

Discussion

Work in pairs.

1 Draw a graph like the one on page 145 to show when the television is on in the speaker's household.
2 Would you say you watched television selectively or indiscriminately? Give examples.
3 Summarise the speaker's views on television for children.

■ Summary ■

Vocabulary

1 Match each expression in the first column with one in the second: what does each pair refer to? TV, radio or newspapers?

a	national	BBC
b	quality	income
c	pop	deregulation
d	daily	local
e	winter	weekly
f	fee	black and white
g	morning	summer
h	ITV	popular
i	colour	evening
j	regulation	serious

2 What are the following and which part of the media are they connected with?
colour magazines   advertisements
tabloids   soap operas   bingo games
Fleet Street   weekend supplements
documentaries   English by Radio
independent production companies
licence fee

Discussion

1 It has been said that 'you can call a popular British tabloid a "paper" but hardly a "newspaper"'. Why do you think this is?
2 Which are the most important newspapers in your country? Describe two of them.
3 How do you think the changes described for radio in Britain will be better for listeners?
4 British TV has been described as 'the least worst TV in the world'. What do you think this description is trying to say?

Writing

Write a paragraph giving your opinion on the advantages and disadvantages of television in modern society.

Filming a TV news item

Views of Britain

■ The official view ■

(What the government would like you to think)

Britain is a stable and democratic society. Its citizens have freedom of speech, and political and religious belief. It is a leading member of both the European Union and the Commonwealth and has a major world role as a permanent member of the United Nations Security Council.

The home of the industrial revolution, it continues to be an important industrial nation. Although small in area and accounting for only about 1 per cent of the world's population, Britain is the fourth largest trading nation in the world. After years of sustained growth it is one of the largest exporters of goods and a major centre for financial and insurance services. It has the largest energy resources of any country in the European Union and is an important world producer of oil, natural gas and coal. Its

labour force has high levels of technical and commercial skill. British agriculture is noted for its efficiency and productivity and at the same time comprehensive planning and control have steadily reduced air and water pollution.

Britain's National Health Service is famous worldwide and its universities and institutes of higher education attract over 50,000 foreign students a year. Britain has for centuries encouraged research and innovation and its record of achievements has been maintained throughout the twentieth century. Nobel prizes for science have been won by sixty-eight British citizens, a number exceeded only by the United States. In the fields of arts, broadcasting and sport Britain continues to lead the world.

Francis Crick and James Watson, Nobel prizewinners
for scientific research

The UN Security Council

The Men's Final at Wimbledon

Rolls-Royce car factory

Comprehension

Use the information on these two pages to answer the questions.

1 Which international organisations is Britain a member of?
2 What examples are given of Britain's industrial power?
3 What evidence is given of Britain's educational success?
4 Name three other areas in which Britain leads the world.

Discussion

Work in pairs.

1 Which do you think are the most important British achievements?
2 Think of three major sports which originated in Britain.
3 Do you find the official view accurate?

■ The people's view ■

Representative of the 'enterprise culture'

How has Britain changed over the past ten years?	
Richer	48%
Poorer	36%
More freedom	44%
Less freedom	24%
More unhappy	48%
Happier	21%
More selfish	61%
More generous	19%
Life is worse	42%
Life is better	39%
A dirtier country	68%
A cleaner country	15%
Less friendly people	52%
Friendlier people	23%
More intolerant	37%
More tolerant	35%
More violent society	59%
Less violent society	12%

Mrs Thatcher created a society which is richer and freer, but also unhappier and more selfish, according to a survey (see above) for the *Observer* newspaper.

People were asked how they thought Britain had changed over the past ten years: 48 per cent thought people were richer, compared with 36 per cent who thought people were poorer. Asked about freedom, 44 per cent thought people now had more freedom, compared with 24 per cent who believed they had less. These positive views of Margaret Thatcher's 'enterprise culture' were balanced by some negative results: 48 per cent thought people were 'more unhappy' today than ten years ago; 21 per cent believed people were 'happier'.

The answers showed considerable differences between various sections of society. Women felt much more strongly than men that life was worse (47 per cent compared with 37 per cent). So did the old (49 per cent) and those living in the north of England (47 per cent).

Graffiti by a racist organisation

Mixed race marriages are increasing

There were a number of reasons for people's opinions. For example, when asked whether Britain was cleaner or dirtier than it had been ten years before, people mentioned an increase in dirt and rubbish in cities and the countryside. People's views on friendliness were influenced by their experience of service industries such as hotels and shops.

The figures on tolerance were more difficult to interpret: some people thought that it referred to racial tolerance and opinion was divided on whether Britain was becoming a more integrated society; others thought that tolerance of political views had declined and that left and right-wing views had become more extreme.

A large majority (59 per cent) believed that Britain had become a more violent society. They pointed to the increase in violent crime (for example, muggings and robberies on the London underground) and the violent reputation of British football supporters.

Comprehension

Use the information on these two pages to answer the questions.

1 According to the survey, what did British people think about:
   a the quality of life?
   b friendliness?
   c generosity?
2 Which sections of society felt more strongly about the decline in the quality of life?
3 On which questions was there a clear majority view?
4 What examples did people give of changes in tolerance and violence?

Discussion

Work in pairs.

1 What do the pictures tell you about life in Britain today?
2 Can you think of any other reasons why people responded to the questions as they did?

■ The Tourist Authority view ■

Tourism is already Britain's fifth most important industry and is also the fifth largest tourist industry in the world. It is growing rapidly: the number of people employed in the industry increased by more than 50,000 a year during the late 1980s. Spending by tourists in Britain in 1985 amounted to £12,000 million, almost half of it by 14.5 million visitors from overseas, and has been increasing since.

Britain has a rich and varied cultural heritage. Colourful royal ceremonies attract millions of visitors each year as do Britain's 450 stately and ancestral homes. London has an international reputation for its historic sites, museums and famous institutions: of these Madame Tussaud's is the most popular, attracting more than two million visitors each year. Historic cities such as Oxford, Cambridge and Bath are visited by large numbers of tourists. People who travel to Scotland, the Lake District and other areas of upland Britain find beautiful scenery which can vary dramatically over short distances. International cultural events such as the Edinburgh Festival attract many visitors.

Some of the most popular attractions to have opened in the 1980s are outside London and include the Jorvik Viking Centre in York, the Tudor ship, the *Mary Rose* Exhibition in Portsmouth and the National Museum of Photography in Bradford, as well as the Burrell Collection in Glasgow and the Albert Dock development in Liverpool. These are in addition to older popular tourist destinations such as Shakespeare's birthplace and the theatre in Stratford-upon-Avon.

The Tower of London

A Tower guard, or Beefeater

Buckingham Palace, the Queen's London residence

Anne Hathaway's cottage, Stratford-upon-Avon

Punting in Cambridge

Morris dancers

The Burrell Collection, Glasgow

Comprehension

Use the information on these two pages to answer the questions.

1 How important is tourism in Britain?
2 What examples are given of tourist sites:
  a in London?
  b outside London?
3 Find examples of the following attractions:
  a a festival
  b a geographical area
  c a new development.

Discussion

Work in pairs.

1 Which of the tourist attractions mentioned would you be most interested in?
2 What other features of British life would attract tourists?

■ A foreign view ■

Introduction

1 What nationality do you think the speaker is: American, French, German, Italian or Spanish?
2 When do you think she first visited Britain: 1937, 1947, 1957, 1967 or 1977?

Listening

Listen and see if you were right. Now answer these questions.

1 Why did she first visit Britain?
2 What sort of training did she take?
3 What does she like about Britain?
4 What does she dislike?
5 What comparisons does she make with other countries?
6 What does she think of Mrs Thatcher?
7 What other immigrants to Britain does she mention?
8 What were they asking for?

Discussion

Work in pairs.

1 Do you think you would enjoy living in Britain? What advantages and disadvantages would there be?
2 Do you agree that 'the Brits are a strange race'? What, if anything, is 'strange' about them?
3 The speaker says, 'In Rome, do as the Romans do.' Do you agree that immigrants to a foreign country should adapt to all the local habits? Or should the country change some of its rules to accommodate immigrants' views?

■ Summary ■

Vocabulary

1 Which of the following words are used positively, and which negatively, in the unit?
   leading   stable   dirty   integrated
   violent   selfish   tolerant   varied
   friendly   extreme   generous   decline

2 Which of the following do you associate most closely with Britain's reputation?
   enterprise   heritage   friendliness
   mugging   pollution   innovation
   democracy

Discussion

1 Find any points which are mentioned in both 'The Official View' and 'The People's View'. Is there any contradiction between them?
2 Which of the four views in this unit tells you most about life in Britain?
3 In your experience what are the main reasons that people visit Britain? How many are mentioned in this unit?

Writing

Choose one of the views of Britain. Find evidence in other units to support or oppose the view you have chosen.

Young people by Piccadilly Circus, London

Appendix

■ Transcripts of Interviews ■

■ UNIT 1 ■

Part 1

. . . I first went into the wildest part of the kingdom, which is Scotland, and the West Coast in particular. I made something of a detour to take in the West Coast, famous for its lochs and mountains, and a wonderful ground for sailing as well as walking. And then I came down to Glasgow, a great city, famous once for its shipbuilding, now much declined, and as I had an interest in that famous figure in English, or should I say Scottish, design, Charles Rennie Mackintosh, I visited of course the School of Art in Glasgow, which he designed.

However, I couldn't linger too long. I had to press on, because Land's End is a long way away. So down I came . . . down into England, and made a little detour to the left, or to the west, into the Lake District, home of Wordsworth, and also home of rain. Home too of midges. But the sun shone, and I pressed on, thinking of my native land, Wales, which calls for another detour to the west.

So down we came to Wales and of course that called for a visit to Snowdon. Climbed in the inevitable rain and mist, but the clouds did roll back for wonderful views down to the island of Anglesey.

Then back into England, picking up the River Severn, which runs down to the sea in the Severn Estuary. That had to be crossed, before getting down to that other western peninsula, which contains another wild landscape of Exmoor and Dartmoor. And here for a time I exchanged my legs for a pony, because pony 'trekking', as it's called, is very popular in Exmoor and Dartmoor. And that helped me on the final stages of my journey, until finally I stood at Land's End, and looked out to the west, knowing that there was nothing but sea between me and New York.

Part 2

Now if you had to do this journey by road, it would of course be another matter . . . you could probably pick up the motorway network at Glasgow, and soon be bowling along at a comfortable seventy miles an hour. Now what is that in kilometres? I'm not quite sure. 110, is it? 110 kilometres an hour?

And down over Shap Fell, which is a pass for the railway and road and then pick up the motorways, of which we were rather late in the field building, but which are now quite a comprehensive network. And the M6 would take you down to the south and then skirting round the great industrial conurbation of Birmingham, by the M6 and joining the M1 which was the original motorway, now in a deplorable condition, which would take you down to London and the capital.

Then if you had to go, if you wanted to trace my footsteps and go down to Land's End, there is an excellent motorway, the M4, which would take you down to the West Country via the beautiful old town of Bath. On through Bristol, Exeter, Plymouth, famous for its associations with many seafaring Englishmen, including of course Drake, the defeat of the Spanish Armada, and then on into Devon, and the final stages to Land's End.

■ UNIT 2 ■

I was brought up in Bangor, County Down, which is about fourteen miles from Belfast, just down the coast. I lived there until I was nineteen, with my family. I came over here, to Manchester, to go to university, and I've stayed. I've been here now for sixteen years.

I think, possibly, some people assume that I came over here to get away from the Troubles, because that's all that we see on the news. But my reason for coming was to go to university, and I don't think I would have gone back anyway. I think a lot of people leave to come here to study, or to work. If people have left, it's often because there is very little work in Northern Ireland. There's a lot of unemployment, and it's one of the things that I notice when I go back now.

When I go back, there's not the same sense of – well – I don't know if danger is too strong a word, but certainly when I left, we were very aware of riots and shootings and there's the constant army presence. When I was at school, I have clear memories of having soldiers on every street corner, standing outside every shop, army trucks and tanks in the streets. And we got very used to it. We got very used to living with news of bombings, or hearing them. I can remember sitting counting the bombs going off in Belfast one Saturday night because if the wind was blowing towards our town, you could hear them quite clearly.

And it is strange, but you get used to that. And of course, things have changed a lot now. There's very little of that, very few bombs, despite what we hear on the news, but the legacy is a lot of unemployment. A lot of problems with housing. A general feeling of depression among a lot of people.

I think some of the positive things are that people still retain their hospitality and warmth and optimism and that's very reassuring and encouraging, and when I go home, it's always still nice to go back.

Belfast itself has changed. It's now quite a thriving city centre, with a lot to offer, and a lot of night life and restaurants and other things that certainly weren't there when I left. It's still a very nice place to visit: a lot of beautiful countryside, lots of places to go, walks – it's an extremely nice place to be.

I don't think I'd go back now, permanently, although I have got a lot of friends who are from Northern Ireland who would go back. Except their reasons for not going back are perhaps that they've married people who are English and want to remain here for that reason. I'm quite happy to stay here now, and go back perhaps once a year or so, as I have

been doing, but I wouldn't want to settle there.

I think what I find difficult about the place is that like a lot of places in England, it's very parochial, and attitudes about social things tend to lag, I would say about ten or fifteen years, behind attitudes here on the mainland. And that's big issues like abortion, for example, and smaller things, like attitudes to smoking, or drinking and driving. You notice, from the things that people say when you're there, when you're in Northern Ireland, that their attitudes really haven't changed in the way that English people's attitudes have, perhaps.

■ UNIT 3 ■

Well, I suppose I do approve of the monarchy, of the idea of a monarchy. I used to disapprove of royal families in general. I think now I accept the idea of a royal family, because they can function and operate outside politics. What I mean by that is that they're not going to be touched by political scandal, in the way that a president, for example, might be, President of the United States, for example.

But although I approve of the idea of a monarchy, I don't approve of the monarchy we have in Britain at the moment. I'm against them personally, if you like. I think the problem we have with our monarchy is that they are greedy, I would say. They are lazy. They display their wealth in a very ostentatious and vulgar way. They keep their wealth and their treasures well away from the public. They don't contribute to the public good.

I think I would be in favour of a monarchy of the sort you find in other countries in Northern Europe: in Scandinavia, in Holland, for example, perhaps in Belgium. Because those royal families set a good example. They're modest. They work hard. You know, you hear, in England you hear all the time, 'Oh, don't you feel sorry for the Royal Family. They work so hard.' I simply don't believe this. I would love to swop my job for their job any day. I don't think they work hard.

The other thing that I don't like about our Royal Family is the fact that they now seem to behave in, you know, like actors in a soap opera. That they've become vulgar. They've become popular and at the same time, they've become vulgar. They're not dignified. And I do think that a monarchy, although it should be modest, it should be dignified. And it should set a good example.

Part 1   ■ UNIT 4 ■

Throughout Western Europe there are identifiable regions and peoples who have a cultural identity and who also think of themselves as a political or cultural unit in some sense. And we see our relationship as being conducted with those areas, particularly with Flanders, which is perhaps the most – one of the most developed, closest to us, and obviously with Scotland.

But Scotland, as we are, are of course governed by a territorial department of Whitehall: the Scottish Office and the Welsh Office, which has all, or nearly all, the functions of Whitehall departments except for Defence. Although Scotland has some Home Office functions; we don't have those. But broadly the environment, health, education, housing, local government, roads, transport, most of the economy, agriculture, forestry, national parks: all these and more are in fact run from Cardiff and from Edinburgh. But there is no democratic body which controls that.

Nice story that I had from a recent visit by an inward investor from Japan, who asked, you know, 'Wales. You have this Principality; you have a Prince, but where is the Prime Minister?' And the answer to that, in a sense, is of course the 'Prime Minister' is the Secretary of State for Wales, who has this wide area of responsibility.

. . . we would see our move towards that kind of democratic government paralleled by the move towards regional federation throughout Western Europe. Indeed, the moral would then be that you would have a strengthened European Parliament, a weakened Council of Ministers, and a strengthened regional representation, directly relating to the centres of power in the Community.

And also of course, what is very exciting these days is an opening up of the nationalities and regional question, as addressed in Western Europe, to Eastern Europe and Central Europe, I – obviously we – we have links with Latvia and Estonia and Lithuania. We've exchanged meetings and discussions with various people there, and it's quite clear that the nationalities question, and the question of decentralisation, is the key to the new democratisation in the Soviet Union.

Part 2

But what we've tried to do to deal with that situation as minorities is for us to work together. The Social and Liberal Democrats, the Ulster Unionists as the two biggest minority parties, we will tend to negotiate amongst ourselves. And we have agreed, early on we agreed, that we would have a formal since '84, we've had a formal parliamentary group jointly with the Scottish National Party there's four of them and only three of us which again gives us a perceived position in the Chamber. And it means that we can get called by Mr Speaker at Prime Minister's Questions; we can get called to speak in debates.

What we do, we meet once a week and we select which of us will be the major leading spokesperson on a particular topic, and usually we will get our slot. And of course it's very important, with the televising of Parliament, that that should happen.

Interviewer: Where do you sit?

Well, when I first went there, I was – I asked one of long-serving attendants of the House, and he said, 'If I were you, sir, I would sit there. Those are the rebel benches.' That's behind the Liberals, and in front of the Ulster Unionists. And, of course, since I've been there for quite a long time now, I've sort of progressed up the bench. I'm not yet a Privy Councillor – a Right Honourable – but I only have to defer, in terms of sitting on the bench, to Privy Councillors, who usually sit at the head. Like retired Prime Ministers like Jim Callaghan and people like this.

But one time when we got there very early on, it was so crowded on the bench that one of us ended up sitting in the lap of a Conservative lady who, we didn't know at the time, was able to speak Welsh. And so we made some remarks to each other about this lady, and of course, she understood. And the great lesson was that you can't get away speaking a minority language in the UK Parliament without being understood.

■ UNIT 5 ■

I, well I graduated from university over twenty years ago and the Law Society's examinations were different then. But what has stayed the same is that non-law graduates have to have a certain founding in law before they can qualify, before they can take the final examination which law graduates take. And that has not changed.

One thing that has changed over the years is that local authorities are less prone to finance it now than was the case then. And for example the large London firms will actually pay non-law graduates to take what is now called the Common Professional Examination, it was called Part One in my day, but there is still a significant number of non-law graduates coming into the profession, and that will continue to be the case.

By comparison with other professional people in England and Wales, solicitors are some way down the league in terms of income. I think, I think only, I think that for example dentists, doctors and surveyors are all significantly better off, and accountants too in the recent survey which I didn't read personally, but I heard this on the grapevine.

I think the pro . . . is, one of the things you've got to remember about this is that a very large number of solicitors in England and Wales are in small firms and are self-employed. Their clients are not particularly wealthy people, and one has to look at it in the context that the clients can only afford to pay what their pockets will stand. And therefore no matter how well-qualified or

expert the professional person is, if his paymaster isn't a large multinational corporation, he can't charge the earth, because the client can't afford to pay it. I think that's worthwhile bearing in mind.

. . . there was a client of the firm who lived within walking distance, and so when the post was taken out to be dropped into the box at something like, I don't know, say 4.30 in the afternoon, when the first lot of post went, there was a letter by hand to this particular chap, and it would be dropped in at his shop near to the postbox, and before the girl who had dropped it off could be back at the office, he'd not only opened the envelope and read it but then phoned the chap who'd written it to discuss it with him, all literally within a minute or so of receiving the letter.

And it's not uncommon for the phone to go potty on a Monday morning simply because people have received letters and have thought about it over the weekend and as soon as 9.00 or 9.30 arrives they're on the phone because they feel that it's their privilege to talk about it first thing in the week. And if fifty people do that all at the same time, life isn't too much fun, first thing on a Monday morning, so, I don't know, one can smile about it, but it's not good for the indigestion . . .

■ UNIT 6 ■

. . . people are always very surprised. Either when they've spoken to me on the telephone and then met me, they're often terribly surprised to see that I'm a different colour to white. Or, if people see me and they haven't actually spoken to me. Certainly I found this when the children were young and I used to go to toddler group. And living in a town like Thame, which is very small and very English, there are hardly – well, certainly when we first moved here, I was, I think I was the only coloured person in the town.

. . . and what I found was, when I went to toddler-group sessions, I'd be the only coloured person there. And before people actually spoke to me, I found people were very wary. A lot of people wouldn't speak to me simply because they felt, I don't know, maybe they felt threatened, or didn't know whether I would have a strong accent, or weren't quite sure what sort of person I would be. It was only until they actually heard me speaking and realised I was just as English as they are that I made friends. But I found it difficult to start with, to make friends.

But the other curious thing was that once people actually got to know me and got to know my personality, I find that people quite like the idea of having a coloured friend, because not many people have them round here. So, I mean that's . . . I'm actually popular! Because of it!

. . . this is really funny. I went, I had to do a balloon job. It was for a christening and the family were really terribly working class, and it was their baby's christening. And I arrived on the Sunday, and it was sort of lunchtime, and I was setting up all these balloons for a christening and the mother came out, the mother of – the grandmother, so to speak.

She came out and she said to me, 'Are you hungry, love?' And I said, 'Oh no, I'm fine.' She said, 'Do you want a bun?' And I thought she meant a sort of currant bun, you know, one of these currant toasted-teacake things. And I said, 'Oh no, honestly, I'm fine.' And she said, 'It's just that I wasn't sure if you ate ham.'

And I realised that she obviously thought I was a Hindu or a strict Muslim or something like that! And I said, 'Oh no.' I said, 'Actually my husband's cooking me a leg of pork at home, you know, don't worry about me.' And she said, 'Well I wasn't sure whether you ate ham.'

■ UNIT 7 ■

Well, over the last year, I've gradually started buying household products such as washing-up liquid, washing powder, even toilet rolls, recycling, et cetera, cleaning things generally. I've gradually changed over to all ecologically sound, environmentally sound items. It had to be a gradual changeover, because they weren't readily available to start with, unless you paid quite a lot of money in health shops.

And also I was a little bit wary, to start with, that they wouldn't work as well as the products that you were used to, although that isn't really a very good reason for not changing over. So I sort of tried out washing up liquid to start with. And that sort of went down very well. I was very pleased to find that it worked very well, just as well as the other stuff, so . . .

I think there's a bit of reluctance because of the money side of it. You're paying out a bit more. But I found actually everything works, you know, absolutely fine. And also I think one – if you do pay a little bit more money, you are probably a little more careful about how much you use, so there's that aspect as well. You're much more conscious all round about how you're using things, so . . .

Well, literally, I would say in about the last four months, virtually, something like that (we're in '89 now) there's been this huge sort of interest in green issues. It's headlines in the press, it's on the main news on television. I think even the *Guardian* newspaper's got an environmental section now, which it didn't have a few months ago, for instance. Articles every week in the papers, aren't there, about it?

So consequently, it's been rather good, actually. I think – I suppose if one was being cynical, you could say well, they just – large manufacturers are jumping on the bandwagon for economic reasons, and obviously they are doing it for that reason. But supermarkets are now selling environmentally okay products. Nearly all of them. And especially – I don't know whether I should name names here, but big – very big – chains like Sainsbury's and Tesco's have actually seemed to be doing particularly well in this area.

I've been recycling bottles for about the last year, because in Brighton we've got bottle banks all over the place, so we can do that here. At the moment, the local borough council, who obviously controls the refuge [*sic*] collection in the town, I think they've got plans, I think they want to actually collect recycled goods from houses in the normal refuge collection, weekly collection, as they do in Sheffield. They've got that organised up there. I think one or two other places as well, but Sheffield is the one that everyone knows about.

I think that's the long-term aim. I mean, certainly I'd be very pleased to do that. You know, you have three separate containers. But I can see, logistically, in Brighton it might be – a place like Brighton, which has got lots of multiple dwelling housing with old people, bedsits, students et cetera, and then a high turnover of people – it actually could be quite difficult to organise. Specially when you've got a tiny kitchen or a shed arrangement, and you've got to sort of – and you're an old person living at the top of a building or something, and you've got to sort of lug all the stuff down, I can see it could be quite difficult to organise. But that's the ideal: that's what I would like to do.

UNIT 8

The secondary school I went to was a direct grant grammar school. It was single sex, boys only, and it was a religious school: Roman Catholic.

The whole aim of the school seemed to be to prepare people for university entrance. So there were three streams in each year, but you got a very clear impression that the pupils who mattered for the staff were those in the top stream who were going to go on to university.

It's interesting that there was actually no careers specialist on the staff. If you were going to leave at sixteen after your 'O' levels then you left at sixteen, and people just – the staff just said goodbye and that was it. They were mainly interested as I say in those who were going on to university. In that sense they were successful, and had a very high rate of successful university applications, but I can't say that I look back on my time there with any sense of love at all. It was a very strict school, very rigid timetable, very rigid teaching methods.

The fact that it was single sex I now see was a big disadvantage and the fact I think also that it was, you know, it was a religious school in a sense was a disadvantage as well. I think it was actually a socially divisive institution in many ways.

It helped me get into university. I suppose

I'm grateful to it for that, but when it came to thinking about schools for my own children there were two basic criteria that my wife and I applied. One was that we would not send our children to single-sex schools and secondly we would not send them to religious schools. They both in fact attended state comprehensive schools, the nearest secondary school to where we live, and I think they had much more enjoyable times at school than I did. And my wife feels the same. She went to a similar school to mine, a Catholic religious school for girls.

As I say, it helped me get into university, but that is what it set out to do. It gave us no training for life, shall we say, no advice at all on careers, so we were left entirely to think of that for ourselves.

UNIT 9

Lloyd's is not a company, for a start. A lot of the time it's reported in the press, it's reported as being an insurance company. It isn't. It's an independent – it's a collection of independent 'names', as they're called. The names are the people with the money who put it up for the backing of insurance risks. The risks are written by underwriters, who are either names or not. They don't have to be, and they can accept a risk from a Lloyd's broker. The risk can originate anywhere in the world and can be on anything: it can be on marine risks, it can be aeroplanes, physical risks like factories or buildings, it can be on liability or personal accident. Lloyd's are one of the major insurers of satellites, and the Arianne space programme is mostly insured in Lloyd's, I believe.

They will – their boast is that they can insure anything. And they do insure most things.

It was founded in the 1600s. It was originally a coffee house run by Edward Lloyd, from which it takes its name. And the original basis was that merchants who had cargoes on ships which were travelling all over the world eventually would, would . . . They put together an intelligence system where any news of a cargo that had been lost or sunk or pirated – when any intelligence was received – it would be forwarded to Edward Lloyd's Coffee House and they'd all meet there and they would be able to find out where their cargoes were, if they were coming in. And eventually that evolved into a mutual protection society so that they would insure each other in the event of one person's cargo being lost or stolen or anything. And it's built up from that.

And it was housed in the Royal Exchange for a time and moved two or three times. And the building it's in now was opened about two years ago.

Apart from the move in buildings, it's become far bigger. The number of people operating from Lloyd's, the number of 'syndicates' (which is a collection of names or their agents), the number of syndicates has increased dramatically. The computerisation, although fairly slow to start in Lloyd's, has been expanding rapidly in the last two or three years and now almost every data storage system is computerised rather than paper. Although there are a lot of those still left.

Again, with computerisation, decentralisation is the key. A lot of people don't need to pay the rents that are in the City: they can communicate just as quickly from the suburbs or indeed anywhere in the country. There's no need for anybody to be in the City apart from a few key people. Brokers and underwriters at the moment still need to be in the city because face-to-face contact is the most important part of our job. For accounts, for back-up, for information storage, it's not necessary.

■ UNIT 10 ■

It's a small bookshop in the centre of Brighton. A place called George Street. It's a little bit off the beaten track, not in the main shopping street, because when we were first setting up, we didn't have the money to afford the rent on such premises. We sell books to students of English as a Foreign Language, and teachers in their schools. We've been open for about four years now.

The reason we set up the shop in the first place was because both of us had been teachers for many years and we had the desire to be self-employed rather than working for someone else all the time.

We've just gone from strength to strength, really. It was the first six or eight months [which] were touch and go, trying to get new customers, but now we're very busy. We've got two other people working here.

Setting up the shop in the first place, as with all small businesses was very difficult, because it's sort of Catch 22. You have no financial track record in running a business yourself, so nobody wants to lend you any money. And you've never previously ordered goods on credit from anyone, so nobody wants to supply you any goods on credit.

So the most difficult thing is to get your potential suppliers, in our case educational publishers, to agree to supply you with your opening stock and wait for their money. And the other one is to find some friendly bank manager who's willing to lend you cash at an extortionate rate of interest, which is always the case with business loans.

Having got over those two problems, and found a property that we could operate from, the rest of it seems to have been comparatively easy. The business is going so fast now, we're beginning to wonder whether it's the business which is running us or us running the business. That's the problem.

The other thing is that you don't escape from being told what to do when you become self-employed. Because when you're an employee, your boss tells you what to do. And when you're self-employed, it's your bank manager or your accountant or most of all your customers who tell you what to do. So you still find yourself tipping your cap to someone or other.

■ UNIT 11 ■

I trained as a teacher, and worked as a nursery teacher in London and in Swansea for eight years, and then stopped to have my first child. Ended up having three, so in all spent nine years at home with the children, which I greatly valued. For a long time I didn't consider doing any type of work at all. I felt that their babyhood and infancy was so short and so important and I didn't want to miss any of it at all.

Once my third child, Branwen, went to full-time school, I found that quite devastating for a short while and thought, 'Help! Where do I go from here?' For a while I thought about doing some other career, but teaching is such an ideal one when you have children because of the holidays, and the hours generally fit in very well.

So I went into supply teaching and did bits and bobs really: two days here, two days there, working just odd days. Which was quite good in some ways, but I find it very difficult going into different schools, meeting different situations, and different people all the time.

Then I did some supply work at a school for severely handicapped children. They were quite short-staffed at the time, and asked me to stay on, and I've been there full-time for nearly two years now. This is work that I enjoy very much. At the moment I'm working with a class of severely physically handicapped children, so we do a lot of work about communication. They have charts and do a lot of computer work. None of them can speak, or walk, but they are a very interesting bunch to work with.

Fitting it in with a family has got easier as time's gone on. The children are now aged twelve, eleven and eight, and they're old enough to understand a bit more about it. They understand that I want to do this. They can understand that if we all help on a Saturday morning, we've got the rest of the weekend to go out and enjoy ourselves. Because I refuse to slave all weekend. I still want my weekends. And they are very good about it.

I have a very good back-up help with a friend who, I really couldn't manage without her. She meets the youngest child from school. And she copes if they're ill. And that, I think that's a horrible dilemma all working mothers have to face. If the children are ill, you want to be with them, and it's horrible to have to leave them even if the person you're

leaving them with is very good, and you know they'll be well cared for. I've been lucky in that they haven't had anything seriously wrong. If they went into hospital or something like that then I suppose you'd face it when it comes. You can't realistically sit at home waiting until they're fifteen in case they might be ill for a few days.

I think I've been very lucky, that the whole debate about whether mothers go to work or not – you're very fortunate if you're like me and you could – we could afford for me not to work for a few years and to do both now. I enjoy both very much.

The difficult things are: time – fitting everything in, giving everybody as much time and attention as they need, and tiredness. You do tend to end up a bit exhausted at the end of the day. But I think it's probably worth trying to do both. I think it's important for the children to see that your whole life doesn't revolve around them. I think that can put quite a burden on children, really.

■ UNIT 12 ■

In my retirement, I really have a very good life. I live in a small town. When my husband was alive, we had a much bigger house, of course, for the family, and I sold this and bought a very small cottage. This is a thing that people are often able to do and then they invest the money from the bigger house and that gives me a large part of my income.

The rest comes partly from savings, but we hadn't very many, but partly from a state pension. My own state pension is slightly higher than the average widow's because I'm a war widow. But all women can get a pension when they are sixty if they have been insured in their own right, and men get this at sixty-five. If you go on working till you're sixty-five or seventy, you then get a slightly larger pension.

So I'm fairly comfortably off. Just with my investments and my pension. Quite a lot of people also have a pension in regard of work that they've done, a firm's pension, or a firm's pension of their husband's if they're widows, but I don't.

People very often say that there is really no poverty in this country. This is not true at all. I was a social worker and working, not in a large city, in Cardiff, which is not one of our larger cities. As a social worker I saw the very real poverty that there is. But it is not widespread, and there is a general attitude of 'I'm all right, Jack', and the government itself does tend to play down this, the poverty that exists.

It's much more difficult to manage if you're poor. Being poor is in itself a handicap, because everything costs much more. That sounds paradoxical, but the more you buy things on credit, the more you have to pay for them, and you have to buy things in smaller quantities, perhaps. When you're buying clothes, you buy them of poorer quality, and then they wear our sooner, so that you get into a vicious circle: the poorer you are, the poorer you become.

Now, as to how I spend my time. It goes very quickly. Of course most people spend, I suppose the majority of their time just getting on with living: shopping, cleaning and cooking, ordinary things like that. I have a group of friends with whom I spend quite a lot of time, going out to lunch, going to the theatre, and concerts, things of that kind, and on the useful side, I spend a good many hours, ten, twelve a week perhaps, taping law books and other teaching material for partially sighted students, which makes me feel not as entirely selfish as I might otherwise feel.

■ UNIT 13 ■

I live in a large house in North Kensington, which is a Victorian family house, which has recently been divided into four flats. My husband and daughter and I share one flat, which is on the first floor, which is a very nice two-bedroom flat with a large living room, small kitchen and roof garden at the back.

The house is near to Portobello Road, which is a very nice part of London to live in. In fact I've always thought it's the nicest part of London to live in. And Portobello Road provides the heart to the area. It also has a lot of local amenities which I find very useful: it

has local schools, local parks, and it's very easy access to other parts of London, in fact to everywhere else.

We rent our flat from friends, and our house is slightly unusual in that we know all the other people in the other flats. It's more of a household, rather than separate families living in separate flats. All our front doors are on the latch all the time, and we move up and down into each others' flats and often help each other out with shared child care or shared shopping and generally it's a very nice, friendly household to live in.

Unfortunately the area's changed a lot over the last ten years as accommodation has gone on the market and the property requirements have increased. So what's happened to all these large houses is they've been divided into endlessly decreasing sizes of flats and smaller units, which means that the families in the street have disappeared, and that there's now very few numbers of children in the street. There are young professional couples moving into flats, and perhaps they have one child and then move out of the flats and buy larger flats or houses elsewhere. So the nature of the street has changed from a very friendly community street into a rather cold, expensive property market street with lots of expensive cars outside and I don't like this.

I used to live in South London, in a housing association flat, which was also near a market: Brixton Market. But the atmosphere in South London was very different, because it's a lot more pressured living, there's a lot more traffic, the streets are a lot narrower, and there's generally a poorer atmosphere. People have less money and less advantages in South London than they do in North Kensington. And I found that very pressured living and now I live in North Kensington I wouldn't move back to South London for the world.

■ UNIT 14 ■

I'm a farmer, basically a sheep farmer, but we've also developed a holiday business which really works in the summer, not so much in the winter.

I've had a driving licence since I was seventeen, which is a great many years, now: I won't tell you exactly how many. I probably drive a variable amount each week. Some weeks I'll drive a lot, depending on the nature of the job I'm involved in. Other weeks I'll probably only do perhaps half an hour's driving. Some of it's local driving: going to the shops and buying essential supplies. Some of it's long-distance driving: up to London and back in one day is not unheard of.

I own two normal road vehicles. One's a van, which I use for obvious reasons, and one's a car: a Japanese car. In fact it's a Japanese-Australian crossbred, which I bought very cheaply because no one else wanted it, and I'll probably never be able to sell.

As well as my road vehicles I own two tractors: one a larger tractor and one a very old, but reliable, smaller tractor that I use round the yards. The larger tractor does most of the heavy work. I also, in connection with the holiday business, hire a couple of minibuses every year, as we have a lot of foreign students come over to study English, and we use the minibuses in order to transport them round the countryside, seeing sights and taking them on activities and so on.

I treat my cars very badly indeed. I'm not very interested in washing them. I get someone else to service them now although when I was younger and more enthusiastic I used to service them myself.

The difference between the car I used to have and the car I now have is that the car I now have very rarely breaks down. The car I used to have broke down regularly and in order to take it any distance I'd have to give it a thorough check over. Now, with Japanese engineering you have a car that you don't really think about. You also don't have to 'drive' it: it's no fun to drive, but it's a unit that takes you from A to B, and has no other function, has no character, no charisma, it just works.

British car manufacturing? Well, there's very little to say about it really, is there? They've missed the boat as far as design and engineering features. What they are left with

is a certain kudos, which they're also beginning to lose, as their cars become more standardised and look like every other car on the road.

■ UNIT 15 ■

Well I qualified in the Welsh National School of Medicine in the late Sixties, and I continued to work at the teaching hospital, in the teaching environment. Obviously, medicine there was practised at quite a sophisticated, high-powered level, and whilst there, I was unaware of any inequalities of treatment. I was a young doctor: idealistic, and it wasn't until I moved into the community that I became aware of these deficiencies and inequalities of the medical service that we were delivering.

I think people – patients – are constantly being told, if they're unhappy with the medical care that they're receiving from their doctors that then they're to vote with their feet and move on to a different practice. I think this is all right in theory, but I think it's quite difficult in a small valley environment or in a rural environment. In the inner cities, where there are lots of practices to choose from, then it might be easier to choose a different doctor if you're unhappy with the service that's being delivered.

In London obviously there are plenty of hospitals. Waiting lists are short. Any patient with a problem can be quickly referred by the General Practitioner. And the General Practitioner also has a choice of places to which he can refer a patient. If he's aware that one hospital offers a better service than another for a certain condition, then obviously the patient can be referred there and generally speaking the waiting lists are short.

But of course out of London and away from the teaching hospital environment, away from the larger cities, then obviously this isn't the case and patients may end up waiting a year or two years for a hospital appointment and then may not still be guaranteed the quality of service that they would have received at a teaching hospital at one of the larger hospitals.

If a patient has no alternative other than to rely on the National Health Service, she (he or she) may be referred to a hospital clinic and have to wait at least a year to be seen at an outpatient clinic. She cannot ask to be seen by a specific doctor and after waiting maybe two or three hours in a crowded waiting room, will be seen by maybe a junior member of staff.

I think, as I mentioned earlier, I think it's sad that undoubtedly there are certain places, certain hospitals that are going to be more attractive places for doctors to work. In certain places in South Wales they're desperately short of medical staff. And however much money is pumped into the NHS, I mean, these places are not going to become any more attractive. So there'll always be this inequality of service.

. . . and I think for some, there'll always be a second-class medical service, unfortunately. But if you do pay for your medicine, then you also have to travel for your medicine. I think one of the advantages in paying for your medicine is that you can actually pay for the consultant, you can choose your doctor, you choose the time of your consultation, and I think you, because you're paying, I think it's a quirk really of human nature, because you pay for something, you feel you're getting the best and psychologically I think you feel better as the result of a private consultation. Although maybe the service that you ultimately receive is no better than the service you might have received as an NHS patient. But there's some satisfaction in that you've made the choice, you've gone along and you've paid your money. At the end of the day you may well, or generally do, feel better for it.

But often you have to travel for your private medicine. Private medicine is not on the doorstep. And that's another strange thing, I think. Patients are prepared to travel for private medicine, and don't moan and groan about that. But already I think we're hearing moans about patients at the prospect of patients having to travel for NHS medicine.

■ UNIT 16 ■

I must talk about why people don't go to the theatre in England today, in our time, and I would say first of all it's to do with the rise of other media, particularly film, particularly the cinema, and even more importantly, radio and television, particularly television. So it's a matter of competition, to some extent. I think that's probably the largest, the main reason why people don't go to the theatre very much, is that there's an easy alternative.

And in the past, particularly, although things are changing somewhat now, it was, it was quite a business to go to the theatre. And also there was a sense, there's a sense, it's been understood in Britain that theatre is for a minority part of the population. A certain class of people go to the theatre: middle class, upper middle class, and above. And when England was more class-conscious you could talk about classes like that. And the working class didn't go to the theatre: it wasn't their thing. So that's a change and a difference that we can observe as compared with Shakespeare's day, where we know that the so-called working class would go to the theatre then.

So to some extent there's a class aspect to the whole thing, why people don't go to the theatre. I think putting aside, if one puts aside historical reasons, I think those are the main things, really, it's a question of theatre having developed as a speciality, a leisure activity for a certain class of people. And then the rivalry of the other media coming in, particularly in the twentieth century. And those two factors together lead us to this very small percentage of people that actually go to the theatre.

And I think of those people that go to the theatre, there is – one of the problems of theatre is that it's a very sort of delicate medium, in the sense that if one goes to the theatre and one sees something that one doesn't like, it can be an acutely painful experience, in fact. And it's very easy to put people off theatre. You can go to the theatre maybe for the first time, see something awful, and never want to go to the theatre again.

It's the same experience that people

sometimes have of Shakespeare for the first time. When they come across Shakespeare at school, it's presented to them badly or they're too young to appreciate it, it's a bore, it's a drag, it's a grind, and all they want to do is to get away from Shakespeare for the rest of their lives, which they invariably do. So Shakespeare is intimately connected with theatre, of course. He's at the very heart of our idea in England of what theatre is, and so there's a whole wedge of the population alienated from – just from education itself, through the education process.

That's, on the other hand, if you go to the theatre and see something that is a positive experience, then the chances are you'll be a convert to the theatre, and the chances are it'll be something you'll see from time to time throughout your life.

Now the revolution that's happened in our time in the theatre is that theatre has become rooted in reality, and begins to present all forms of everyday life to people. And so that, I think, that's widened the theatre audience as well. Theatre has become realistic; theatre has become relevant. And this happened in the fifties, with *Look Back in Anger*, Pinter, *The Birthday Party*, plays like that. So there's been a big change.

■ UNIT 17 ■

Well, I suppose that I watch some television most days. My television watching tends to happen late at night for sort of domestic reasons and work reasons, so it's restricted by that, I watch a lot of news programmes, I nearly always watch the news, or current affairs programmes. I'm quite a sports fan as well, so if there's any sport on I tend to watch it: cricket, or football or something like that, if I've got nothing better to do.

I have a daughter who's six, and she watches children's television quite often when she comes back from school. Children's television lasts about an hour and a half. Sometimes she'll sit through right from beginning to end and other times she'll get bored and switch off and go away and do something else.

So in our house the television tends to be on in the late afternoon and late at night. But I'm amazed at figures that I came across recently, for example that some people may watch as much as twenty-eight hours in a week. That was in winter, I think, when the weather's bad and people are inside anyway. I don't know whether that means the time that the television is on or whether people actually watch it for that amount of time, because I think in some homes the television goes on as a kind of background and people don't actually watch it in any kind of concentrated way.

I suppose one of the things that worries me as a parent is the effect that television has on children. I don't take the same view as a lot of friends of mine who think that TV is some kind of danger to them. I think people are very inconsistent here. People never said that radio was a great danger to children, and I don't see any real difference between radio and television in that sense.

I think television can be a great benefit to children. I think there are a lot of good programmes that give them good educational information, presented in a way which is very attractive to them. For example, there's a very good nature programme, which is presented in a very exciting way on television and is very good viewing, and very educational as well. And I also think television's good for introducing children to good literature. There are often children's stories. Good children's stories are dramatised for television and this can often attract children to go and read the book, and I think that's a good thing.

The most dangerous thing, I think, for children on television is the commercialism, and I get really angry about television programmes that are produced, which are really produced not because they're interesting television programmes but because they're part of a big marketing exercise, so that at the same time the shops will be flooded with rubbers and pencils and bags and pencil cases and things like this and there's a tremendous pressure on children to go out and buy those things, and I think that is a very dangerous thing indeed.

The other dangerous thing, I think, for children is if the television is on indiscriminately, then they do, if parents are not careful, they do get to see programmes which are not suitable for them. And I think that is a big danger. But that's up to the parents to make sure that that doesn't happen, I think.

I find it very difficult to say what would be a reasonable time to watch television. I think the important thing is not how much you watch but how selective you are. That you say, this is an interesting programme and worth watching, and I'll watch it, and if there are a lot of good programmes in one week, you might spend quite a bit of time watching television; another week, when the programmes are not so good, far less. So it's very difficult to say, what is a reasonable amount of time.

■ UNIT 18 ■

I first came here in 1947 to stay with friends in Yorkshire and I stayed there for six months, and as I always wanted to become a nurse, I applied to St Thomas's Hospital in London, where I was accepted. I did my nursing training, which I finished in '52. You see?

Well, the Brits are a strange race, but oh, no. There's something marvellous about Britain. Really, yes. Even now things are changing all the time. But I don't say that just because I'm a foreigner. People are very kind on the whole. I mean this is Wales and this is different. North Wales is different from South Wales. But there is a quality of life. Definitely. I love Britain. Really, I love everything about it.

Except perhaps certain aspects of food. You know, after living in Brussels for fourteen years, when one had such a choice of everything, it's sometimes difficult. But it's such a small thing, you know, mind over matter, and it really, it doesn't matter, it really doesn't matter. You know, it's lovely living here.

The good points? Well, there are so many. People are gentle, on the whole. I mean the people I mix with – I deal with. No I don't find much to criticise. I mean if I criticise, it's in a very nice way.

Small things, but I mean for instance in my family, or in France, you always start, say, with soup, or an entrée, and then you . . . different ways of living. You know, just things are different. It's a marvellous country, and I must say, maybe I shouldn't talk politics here, but I must say, thanks to Maggie Thatcher, you know, Britain, is what it used to be. I mean I remember when we went to Brussels in '74, I mean we were almost afraid to say, you know, we came from Britain, because things are . . . but thanks to Maggie Thatcher things have looked up. Of course, I mean it's very controversial I mustn't say a lot about that, perhaps. But I think she's marvellous, I really do.

So. But people are very kind on the whole. Of course you see I am – I mean, we are retired. My husband took an early retirement and perhaps if we were younger . . . I forgot, I forget what it was like perhaps. But people have always been very kind and tolerant, much more tolerant than the French, I think. That's why I get so irritated. For instance the other day I saw on television some, I think they were Pakistani people, parents, in the Midlands somewhere. They wanted, if I heard right, they wanted a teacher to teach their children in their own language. Well, this is Britain, surely. You must do, you know, and live . . . In Rome, do as the Romans do, surely. You can't just have your own way all the time, can you? Oh no, that won't do. No.

Web Addresses

BUBL UK: *http://www.bubl.ac.uk/uk*
BUBL (pronounced 'bubble') is based at Strathclyde University in Glasgow. Its information is organised in the same way as a traditional library, following the Dewey system. This means that related information is found together 'on the same shelf'. If you prefer this system of organisation to search engines, BUBL is for you. BUBL UK takes you to its UK resources. For example you can find today's news stories about the themes in this book, or compare the British newspapers described in Unit 17 'The Media' at:
http://www.bubl.ac.uk/uk/newspapers.htm

National Statistics: *http://www.statistics.gov.uk*
This is the UK government's official site for statistical information. For example, the annual report *Social Trends* was used extensively in the preparation of this book, particularly Unit 12 'The Cost of Living'. It can be downloaded from this site: click on 'Bookshelf'.

BBC: *http://www.bbc.co.uk*
The BBC site is as rich and varied as the BBC's television and radio services. It provides up-to-date news coverage as well as clearly organised information in other areas. For example, click on 'History' under 'Categories' on the front page and you will find material about the nations of Britain described in Unit 2 'The United Kingdom'.

British Library: *http://www.bl.uk*
This is the modern catalogue of the old British Museum Reading Room. There are interesting exhibitions on its home page. It has a very attractive section full of ideas for projects for schools and colleges. For example, at the time of writing it has a project called 'The Making of the UK' which goes into the historical background to Unit 2 of this book in interesting detail. Look at:
http://www.education.bl.uk

British Tourist Authority: *http://www.visitbritain.com*
The BTA site is designed to attract visitors to Britain and its context is described in Unit 18. It currently has a 'Virtual Journey' through the British countryside, which will add to your enjoyment of Unit 1. If you want to see what cultural and sporting events are happening at the moment, try:
http://www.visitbritain.com/uk/events/events.htm

UK Online: *http://www.ukonline.gov.uk*
By 2005 all UK government offices will be represented on this site. Its main aim is to provide internet access to government services for UK citizens, but it also leads you to an enormous range of information about British government through its excellent search engine. Click on 'Newsroom' for a current list of hot topics. For instance, at the time of writing, they featured a story about marriage and divorce in Britain, which was very relevant to Unit 11.

Schoolsnet: *http://www.schoolsnet.com*
This is a commercial site that provides information about schools but it also has excellent services for schoolchildren and students. Click on 'Lessons' on the home page and look for topics of relevance to this book. For example, they currently have a project called 'Systems of government' which would be relevant to Unit 3 page 20. This is designed for students at Key Stage 3 (see page 63). Or click on 'Webguide' for a selection of other web-based resources that can be used in schools and colleges.

Other internet resources
General search engines such as Google were immensely helpful in revising this book. Click on 'Language Tools' on your local Google home page to narrow your search to websites in English and/or based in the UK or go straight to the UK Google home page at:
http://www.google.co.uk

General reference tools are also invaluable. The bookshop Bibliomania has a reference section that has almost replaced our shelves of reference books at home. Click on 'Research' at:
http://www.bibliomania.com

170

List of Maps, Diagrams and Figures

1 The Geography of Britain

Page
The British Isles: physical 5
Europe: population 6
The British Isles: population 7
Annual/monthly rainfall 8
Farmland/How farm work has changed 9

2 The United Kingdom

The British Isles: political 13
The British Isles: population (by country) 13
Indo-European languages 15
Religion in Ireland 17

3 The Constitution

The system of government 21
How Bills go through Parliament 22/23
The Royal Family 25

4 Politics

Voting changes since 1945 29
Changes in government spending 31
General Election 33

5 The Law

The legal system in England and Wales 37
Police stop and search 39
Offences recorded by the police 40
Average prison population in Great Britain 41

6 Britain and the World

The Commonwealth 44/45
Immigrants permitted to settle 46
Ethnic groups 46
Languages in London schools 46
Economic status by sex and race 47
The European Union 49
Visits to and from UK 50
The Channel Tunnel route 50/51

7 Energy and the Environment

Conservation and threat/Protected land 55
Concern about the environment 57
Electricity generation 58/59

8 Education

The school system in England and Wales 63
Students in further and higher education 66
Young people in education 66

9 Business and the Economy

The second industrial revolution 71
Industries privatised between 1979 and 1989 72
Shareholders 73

10 Employment

Social classes 79
The working population 80
New jobs 81

Notes for Teachers

Aims of the book

The aim of *Britain Explored* is to provide a variety of detailed background information on modern Britain, and to present this information through a combination of text and diagrams. The skills that students practise in using such a book will include interpretation and discussion as well as a range of reading skills. Listening practice is provided through the authentic interviews for each unit. The book is designed to be used by students whose English language level is at least intermediate.

The book is intended mainly for students who are engaged in courses such as British Life and Institutions, or British Background and Cultural Studies. However, it is hoped that the information contained in the book will be of interest to a wide range of students, and although the book is primarily aimed at the classroom, it is also possible for it to be used on an individual self-study basis. The book provides the basis for 80–100 hours of work.

Format

The book is divided into eighteen units, each one dealing with a separate topic of information about Britain. Although the book is designed to be worked through in chronological order, the units are more or less self-contained and can therefore be re-ordered to fit with a different syllabus, for example where an institution is already using a topic syllabus and wishes to fit different units into it.

Each unit is divided into five sections: the usual unit format is three double-page spreads, each on a topic or topics related to the theme of the unit, followed by a page for the unit interview and a summary page designed to review some of the information and vocabulary contained in the unit and to provide a basis for writing practice. Most of the units are eight pages in length. There are comprehension and discussion questions for the various sub-sections of each unit.

A major feature of the book is the use of a wide variety of diagrams. These include maps, charts, figures and graphs: a full list is given on pages 170–71. As much of the information in the book is in non-text form, it will be necessary with some classes to spend time ensuring that the students know what exactly each diagram is designed to show. The diagrams provide considerable opportunity for oral work, including description and discussion, and in order to make the best use of the book students should be encouraged to ask questions and to talk about the diagrams and the information they contain.

Guidelines

The method of working through a unit will depend on a number of factors, including the time available and the level of the class. However, a basic methodology would include some or all of the following:

☐ The photographs on the first page of the unit can be used as an introduction; they are designed to set the scene and to provide a background for the information to follow. They can be used for some basic vocabulary work, or for a brief introduction by the teacher, or for students to make comparisons between different photographs. Other photographs throughout the units can be used in a similar way to complement the information from texts and diagrams.

☐ The reading text on the first page sets out some basic information with more information on the topic being provided by a diagram or diagrams. Students need to understand the main details and vocabulary of the text and also to understand what the diagram shows. The comprehension questions on the first double-page spread relate to the information from the text/diagrams on those two pages but there are more questions which could be asked and more time can be spent on exploiting the texts if this is required. A basic technique for the diagrams is to get students to describe what the diagram is about and to encourage them to pick out some of the details to illustrate the main theme. There is considerable scope for practising the use of numbers and figures and also for making comparisons and talking about statistics.

☐ Opportunities are provided for information on the student's own country to be used for comparison. While students' awareness and knowledge of the systems which operate in their own countries will vary considerably, it is recommended that where possible an element of comparison is introduced. This could involve students in work outside the class and could be incorporated into various forms of project work.

☐ The discussion questions can be approached via pairwork, as suggested in the text, or they can be done individually with students then comparing answers. Pair or groupwork is also possible with the comprehension questions. Again the questions provided do not cover all the points of information contained on those two pages and there is scope for more questions if these are required. The format is designed to give an opportunity for a widening of the topic area and a discussion of possible issues raised by the information contained in the unit. As it stands most of the exploitation is designed for oral answers but it is, of course, possible for answers to the comprehension and discussion questions to be used for writing practice.

☐ The listening section (interview) can be done as suggested in the unit format, i.e. with pre-questions followed by questions on the interview itself and then discussion points. Students should be allowed to listen to the tape at least twice and for lower ability groups it may be necessary to divide the listening into shorter sections and to repeat the tape several times.

☐ All the units can be supplemented with additional material. Suitable websites are described on page 169. These will lead you to printed resources as well. Apart from adding interest and variety, additional statistical material can be used to see how the figures change over time. News stories illustrate the general trends described in this book. Sources in your own country will help students to make comparisons between UK data and local data. Educational websites may also give you extra ideas for presenting and developing the information in this book.

Sources of Information

The text sources of information consulted in the compilation of this book include:

Britain: An Official Handbook, annual publication, Central Office of Information, HMSO, London.

Bromhead, P 1985 *Life in Modern Britain* Longman, London.

Economic Trends, annual publication, Central Statistical Office, HMSO, London.

Fothergill, S and Vincent, J 1985 *The State of the Nation* Pan, London.

Key Data 1987 and 1988, HMSO, London.

Regional Trends, annual publication, Central Statistical Office, HMSO, London.

Room, A 1986 *Dictionary of Britain* OUP, Oxford.

Sampson, A 1983 *The Changing Anatomy of Britain* Hodder, London.

Social Trends, annual publication, HMSO, London.

The *Economist*, weekly magazine, London.

The *Guardian,* daily newspaper, London.

The *Independent*, daily newspaper, London.

The *Observer*, weekly newspaper, London.

Whitaker's Almanack, annual publication, Whitaker, London.

Pearson Education Limited
Edinburgh Gate, Harlow
Essex CM20 2JE, England
and Associated Companies throughout the world

www.longman.com

© Longman Group UK Limited 1992
© Pearson Education Limited 2002

The right of Paul Harvey and Rhodri Jones to be identified as authors of this Work has been asserted by them in accordance with the Copyright, Designs and Patents Act 1988.

First published in 1992.
This new edition published 2002.

Set in 10/11pt Century

Printed in Spain by Mateu Cromo

ISBN 0582 47974 6

The Publishers have adapted material from the following sources: p.6 Whitaker's Almanack 2001, pp.790–794, J Whitaker and Sons Ltd London; p.8 (left) Ordnance Survey Atlas of Great Britain 1982, p.11, Ordnance Survey and Country Life Books (Hamlyn) London, and Stamp, L Dudley 1960 Britain's Structure and Scenery fig. 3 p.34, Fontana (Collins) London, (right) Whitaker's Almanack 1988, p.63, J Whitaker and Sons Ltd London; p.9 Graves, NJ and White, JT 1976 Geography of the British Isles (4th edn.) Heinemann Educational Books; p.13 Whitaker 2001 pp.793–794; p.14 Padfield, Colin F 1983 British Constitution Made Simple (6th edn.) p.350, Heinemann Educational Books; p.15 Stevenson, Victor (ed.) 1983 Words, an Illustrated History of Western Languages pp.12–13, Book Club Associates/Macdonald and Co; p.17 Dewar, Michael 1985 The British Army in Northern Ireland p.165, Arms and Armour Press; p.21 Whitaker 2001; p.25 Today 27th February 1989, The Independent 24th December 1987 and Whitaker 2001; p.29 Henig, S and Baston, L (eds) 2000 Politico's Guide to the General Election, Politico's London, and Whitaker's Almanack 1998, J Whitaker and Sons Ltd London; p.31 Social Trends No. 31, Government Statistical Service (HMSO); p.32 Brighton Pavilion Conservative Association 19th February 2001 and http://www.labour.org.uk 25th March 2001; p.33 Henig and Baston 2000; p.34 Whitaker 1998; p.39 Social Trends No. 31 and The Independent 1st March 2001; p.40 Social Trends No. 31 and The Independent 27th February 2001; p.41 Social Trends No. 19; pp.44–5 Whitaker 2001; p.46 (top) Social Trends Nos. 30 and 31, (bottom left) Social Trends No. 31, (bottom right) ILEA survey 1988; p.47 Social Trends No. 18; p.49 Whitaker 2001 p.780; p.50 Social Trends No. 31; p.55 Britain 1984, an official handbook 1984, Central Office of Information (HMSO), Britain 1987, an official handbook 1987, Central Office of Information (HMSO), Ordnance Survey Atlas of Great Britain 1982, pp.172–3, North Sea or Dead Sea? The Sunday Telegraph weekend magazine and Social Trends No. 19; p.57 Social Trends No. 18; p.58 Social Trends No. 31; p.63 Social Trends No. 19, Chapter 3; p.66 (left) Social Trends No. 30, (right) Social Trends No. 31; p.68 Parents' Concerns Which? May 1988; p.71 Social Trends No. 19; p.73 Social Trends No. 19; p.80 Social Trends No. 31; p.81 Social Trends No. 31 and The Guardian 17th February 2001; p.82 (both) Social Trends No. 31; p.84 (left) Social Trends No. 31, (right) Charterhouse Guide to top management remuneration in UK 1986–7, New Earnings Survey 1986, HMSO, and Regional Trends 1986, HMSO; p.85 source unknown, footnote (A) Department of Education 18th September 1986; p.89 (all) Social Trends No. 19; p.90 (both) Social Trends No. 31; p.91 source unknown; p.96 Social Trends No. 31; p.97 (top) Social Trends No. 19, (bottom) Social Trends No. 31; p.98 (top) The Independent 8th March 2001, (bottom) Social Trends No. 30; p.100 (top left and right) Social Trends No. 31, (bottom) Social Trends No. 30; p.101 (both) Social Trends No. 31; p.105 (both) Social Trends No. 19; p.109 Social Trends No. 31; p.114 (both) Social Trends No. 31; p.116 The Guardian 24th June 2000; p.118 ACI http://www.airports.org; p.119 Whitaker's Almanack 1973, p.596, J Whitaker and Sons Ltd London, and Whitaker 1988, p.606; p.123 (top) Timmins, Nicholas (ed.) 1988 Cash, Crisis and Cure, The Independent Guide to the NHS Debate, Newspaper Publishing plc., (bottom) Social Trends No. 19; p.124 Eurostat Yearbook 2000; p.125 Social Trends No. 19; p.126 (top) caption from Social Trends No. 19, (bottom) Social Trends No. 19; p.127 Social Trends No. 19; p.131 (bottom left) Social Trends No. 17, (right) Social Trends No. 19; p.132 Social Trends No. 19 and New Society Database 2nd April 1988; p.133 Social Trends No. 31; p.135 Social Trends No. 31; pp.136–7 New Society Database 29th April 1988; p.141 The Guardian 14th August 2000; p.142 (top) Social Trends No. 19, (bottom) Social Trends No. 31; p.145 (top) Social Trends No. 19, (middle) Social Trends No. 17; p.150 The Observer survey.

Acknowledgements

The authors would like to acknowledge the considerable contribution of all the speakers on the student cassette, and in particular to note with great sorrow that both John Nuttall of Exeter University (page 68) and Bronwen Jones, formerly of Dolgellau, North Wales (page 102), passed away shortly before this edition was published.

We are grateful to the following for their permission to reproduce photographs and other copyright material:

Allsport UK Limited for page 133 (middle and bottom). Argos Distributors Limited for page 103. Art Directors & TRIP for pages 81, 134 (top) and 139 (middle). The Bank of England for page 74 (left). John Birdsall Photography for pages 65 (left), 93 (top left and top middle) and 140 (middle and bottom). Nick Birch for page 65 (right). The British Council for page 143. British Rail for page 112. CADW for page 15. Camera Press for pages 40, 51 (top) and 83. The J. Allan Cash Photolibrary for pages 61, 67 (right), 90 (left), 108 (top left), 122, 133 (top), 135 (top and bottom left), 139 (top), 150 (bottom), 153 (bottom left and bottom right). Docklands Corporation for page 108 (bottom right). Dominic Photography for page 135 (bottom right). Greg Evans International for pages 4 (bottom left), 36, 45, 62 (right), 93 (top right), 106 (middle right), 107 (bottom left), 117 (middle), 119, 126 (top left and right), 135 (middle), 151, 152 (top right) and 153 (top left and right). Mary Evans Picture Library for page 12 (middle). Eye Ubiquitous/Derek Redfearn for page 39 and /David Cumming for page 53. Faulds Advertising Limited/Meiklejohn for page 73 (bottom right). Forestry Commission for page 56 (top left and right). Getty Images for pages 69, 70 (right), 77, 88 (right), 95, 121 and 147. Sally & Richard Greenhill for pages 38 (left), 48 (bottom left), 70 (bottom left), 78 (left and right), 90 (left), 92 (middle), 93 (middle middle and bottom left) and 142. Greenpeace/Menzel for page 56 (bottom right) and /Zindler for page 57. Ideal Homes for page 108 (middle). ImageState for page 150 (top). Impact Photos/Philippe Achache for page 25, /John Arthur for page 38 (left and middle), /Piers Cavendish for page 62 (left), /Homer Sykes for page 93 (bottom right) and /Julian Calder for page 106 (middle left). International Stock Exchange Photo Library for page 74 (right). Katz FSP for page 96 (left and right) and /R. Nightingale for page 35. The Labour Party for pages 30 (left) and 32 (left). Life File for page 93 (middle right) and /Nicola Sutton for page 79 (bottom left). Billie Love Historical Collection for pages 88 (left) and 144 (left). M&S Chargecard for page 100 (right). Midland Bank plc for page 100 (left and middle). Mirror Syndication International for pages 14 (top and bottom), 54, 56 (bottom left), 99 (left), 108 (top right), 109, 118 (middle) and 149 (bottom left). Network Photographers/Spraham for page 92 (bottom), /Sturrock for pages 108 (bottom left) and 111 and /Franklin for page 129. PA Photos for pages 27 and 28 (top). The Photo Library Wales for page 14 (bottom right). Pictor International for pages 11, 99 (right), 130 and 155. Popperfoto for pages 24 and 44. Power Pix for page 48 (top right). Rex Features for pages 12 (left and right), 50, 51 (middle), 87, 115 (bottom), 134 (bottom right) and 137 (bottom right). Rolls-Royce Motor Cars Limited for pages 115 (top left) and 149 (bottom right). Rover Group for page 115 (top right). The Scout Association for page 93 (middle left). Supercar & Classics for page 136–7. Topham Picturepoint for pages 14 (top right) 20, 144 (right), 148 (left) and 149 (top). Universal Pictorial Press & Agency for pages 28 (bottom) and 117 (top). University of Sussex for page 67 (left). Viewfinder for pages 107 (top right) and 118 (top). What Hi-Fi Magazine for page 136–7. Zefa Picture Library for pages 4 (top left and right, and bottom right), 22, 23, 48 (top left, middle left and middle right), 58, 59, 75 (right), 79 (top right, middle left, middle middle, middle right and bottom right), 104, 106 (bottom left), 107 (top and middle left), 134 (bottom left), 139 (bottom) and 152 (top left and bottom).

All other photographs supplied by Rhodri Jones.

Cover photographs: top left – Format Photographers; top middle – Corbis/Jeremy Horner; top right – Pictor International; bottom left – Image Source; bottom right – Getty Images.

Picture Research by Louise Edgeworth.

Designed by Sylvia Tate.

Artwork by Stuart Perry and Oxford Designers and Illustrators.